Good Questions

Answering Letters From the Edge of Doubt

For Denise

Blessings & Peace!

Thomas W. Shepherd, D. Min.

TW Shepherd

Good Questions

Answering Letters From the Edge of Doubt

First edition 2009

To place an order, call the Customer Care department at 1-800-669-0282 or go online at *www.unity.org*.

Cover design by Doug Brown
Interior design by Covington Group

Library of Congress Control Number: 2009931129
ISBN: 978-0-87159-329-0
Canada BN 13252 0933 RT

unity®
HOUSE

Good Questions:

Answering Letters From the Edge of Doubt

First edition 2009

To place an order, call the Customer Care department at 1-800-669-0282 or go online at *www.unity.org*.

Cover design by Doug Brown
Interior design by Covington Group

Library of Congress Control Number: 2009931129
ISBN: 978-0-87159-329-0
Canada BN 13252 0933 RT

David said, "What have I done now? It was only a question."

— 1 Samuel 17:29 (NRSV)

For the Rev. James A. Pearce (1953–2009),

Unity Institute's first Master of Divinity graduate,

who always asked good questions

and taught his faculty and fellow students

what kindness looks like

when it's smart and inquisitive.

Acknowledgements

Many thanks to the faculty, staff and students at Unity Institute®, the folks at Unity House, the whole Unity Village community and my friends at the Association of Unity Churches International for their encouragement and confidence in the value of this project. I would also like to thank some influential friends, ministers, spiritual guides and teachers who have helped me along the path, none of whom should be held accountable for anything I said in this volume. Listed in approximate chronological sequence through my life, they are Harry Keim, Gerald W. Jarsocrack, G. Richard Ott, Dawn Edwards, Arthur Dahl, Dwight Allen, Marcus Bach, William Sears, Oliver Reed Whitley, Dana Wilbanks, James C. Lewis, Richard Henry, Robert Eddy, James D. Glasse, Richard F. Veith, Robert Payson, James Dillet Freeman, Donald R. Jennings, Norman Vincent Peale, Ed Rabel, Philip White, Wayne and Janet Manning, Robert Hungerford, Marilyn Roth, Elayne Demetreon, Robert Gillespie, Phillip and Dorothy Pierson, Ruth Langdon, Bhante Wimala, John Shelby Spong, Lynne Brown, Matthew Fox and Bart Ehrman. I would be remiss if I did not also mention the living legend whose office door is a few steps from mine, the granddaughter of Charles and Myrtle Fillmore, my friend Rev. Rosemary Fillmore Rhea.

I am grateful to the great treasure of my life, my best friend and life-mate, Carol-Jean, who allowed me to take over the dining room table *one more time* while working through this mammoth project. Proverbs 3:15 applies. (All you romantics go look it up.)

One final "Thank you" to my readers, especially those who have come up to me through the years at lunchtime in the Unity Inn, or at retreats or workshops and said, with a look of genuine affection, "You know, your column is the first place I turn when the new issue of *Unity Magazine* arrives." And usually I will reply, with deep humility and metaphysical gratitude, "Me too."

Well, it's good to know at least two of us are reading this stuff ... Blessed are those who hunger and thirst after theology. God loves us too.

Contents

Foreword

In June of 1891 the first issue of *Unity Magazine* was published in Kansas City, Missouri. It was created by my grandfather, Charles Fillmore, who with my grandmother, Myrtle Fillmore, founded the Unity School of Christianity as a movement dedicated to prayer, religious education and spiritual healing. Charles was then a 36-year-old man who had embarked on a spiritual quest. By publishing this magazine he hoped to inspire others to join with him in exploring new dimensions of thought. He felt that our search for enlightenment must take us beyond the rigidity of orthodoxy into the uncharted frontiers of consciousness. He wrote: "The need to know and understand is critical. We can afford to make any sacrifice to bring about the development of the pearl-of-great-price spiritual understanding."

Charles Fillmore truly enjoyed dialoguing with others on the quest and published articles by many well-known spiritual writers. Sometimes he included his own ideas at the beginning and end of the article. He also wrote an original column called "Question and Answers." Today, more than a century later, "Question and Answers" has become "That's a Good Question," written by Dr. Thomas Shepherd, and is the most popular feature of *Unity Magazine*.

It is interesting that the two spiritual sojourners who have followed my grandfather in answering the questions asked by readers found their way to Unity through their desire to explore new ideas, to experience beyond the theological theories as taught by the more traditional Christian community. These two remarkable men, although quite different in many respects, share the same inquisitive, restless spirit that moved through my grandfather.

The first to come was Dr. Marcus Bach, a professor of religion at the University of Iowa. He was also a spiritual researcher and a writer of books about new American religions. Marc traveled the world in search of people whose mystical experiences had led them into new dimensions. Marc became a good friend of mine, and I discovered that nothing was beyond his interest. When he spoke, whether it was about walking by the Ganges River with a Hindu holy man or attending a voodoo ceremony in Haiti, you went there with him. Listening to Marc always transported me to new, mysterious worlds.

Marcus Bach first came to visit Unity in 1942, when its headquarters was still in Kansas City. At that time he was just beginning his career in religious research, which was to evolve into his life work. He was raised in the American version of the German Evangelical Church, which after several mergers became the United Church of Christ. He had actually been ordained in the Evangelical church and had served as a minister for one year before deciding that, as he explained, "I realized I had misread my calling. My interest was deferential, more centered in a curiosity about what others believed and why they believed it rather than in converting anyone to a single sectarian expression."

Marc's quest for truth took him around the globe and inspired him to write many books about the "mysterious, magnificent, venturesome world of religions." However something kept bringing him back to Unity, perhaps because he found the same kind of ecumenical acceptance and inquisitive open-mindedness which he developed as a scholar of many religious traditions. In 1962 he wrote *The Unity Way of Life* and in 1982 revised it as *The Unity Way*. Because of Marc's knowledge of world religions, the editor of *Unity Magazine* thought Marc would be the ideal person to answer readers' questions about their spiritual journey.

Marc lived in California and wrote his column "Questions on the Quest," until a year before his death in 1995. Marc was never a member of a Unity church, and I think he always believed that he belonged to the denominational church of his birth, but in a spiritual sense he was completely eclectic. His mind and spirit could not be limited by doctrines that refused to acknowledge that there were many paths to God and the search itself is the greatest adventure of all.

After Marc retired from *Unity Magazine* in 1994, another amazing man moved into the vacancy and brought with him a résumé as diverse and as adventuresome as Marc's had been. This person was Thomas Shepherd, the author of this book and the person who has followed my grandfather and

Marcus Bach in answering questions asked by readers of his column in *Unity Magazine* called "That's a Good Question."

I became a fan of Tom's long before I met him in person. I was always impressed how eloquently he responded to the hard questions that required thoughtful, inspired answers. Like Marc, Tom came from another German-American family and describes himself as "Pennsylvania Dutch." His first career path took him into military service. In Vietnam he became a decorated medical evacuation helicopter pilot. After the war he left the military to earn a B.S. Ed. (*cum laude*) at the University of Idaho and then attended Lancaster Theological Seminary where he graduated *magna cum laude* with a Master of Divinity degree. He then returned to his military career and completed 20 years as an Army Chaplain. After leaving the military, his quest led him to Unity and in 1989 he became a Unity minister and served as senior minister of Unity churches in Georgia, South Carolina and California. In Georgia, he also served as assistant executive director and theologian-in-residence for Johnnie Coleman's Universal Foundation for Better Living.

Now Tom is chair of Historical and Theological studies in the Ministry and Religious Studies department of Unity Institute, located at Unity Village, Missouri. It was here that I finally got to know Tom, and I discovered he was as interesting in person as he is in his column. Tom and his lovely wife, Carol-Jean, have become my good friends, and we are blessed to have them at Unity Village. The military career that took Tom around the world, coupled with his keen mind, has made him an outstanding historical theologian and prepared him to be the perfect heir to follow Charles Fillmore and Marcus Bach in answering the challenging questions that spiritual seekers ask as they go forward on their journey.

One of the nicest things for me, having spent my life in Unity, has been knowing the exceptional people who have come to Unity Village at just the right moment to join with those who came before us and bring their passion, talents, intellectual wisdom and spiritual insight to move us ever forward on the quest. It is always a joy to talk with Tom because he is so open to other new ways of thinking and so very knowledgeable about the world of religion. I often think when visiting with him how fortunate his students are to have such a wise scholar as their teacher and how we are so blessed to have his insightful answers to "That's a Good Question" in every issue of *Unity Magazine.*

Since *Unity Magazine* was first published, amazing changes have occurred in our world. Science and technology have led us into incredible dimensions of new possibilities. People have walked on the moon; robots roam Mars. The communications revolution, globalization of commerce, and the speed of travel have made us a global society whether we like it or not. The prognostications as we move further into the 21st century seem to go beyond even our science fiction fantasies. However, the ageless questions that have perplexed humankind throughout the centuries are still asked today:

Good Questions
⌒

What is the meaning of life? Why do we suffer? What happens after we die? Questions like these have puzzled great minds through the ages and have been addressed by the many different world religions. Today quantum physicists are exploring the nature of energy as related to consciousness. My grandfather believed it was possible to find a bridge connecting science and religion, which would eventually bring forth a "new heaven and earth."

I know if you are reading this book you are a kindred spirit, joining with all who have brought us to this amazing moment. And perhaps, as we continue our search for answers, we will discover a magnificent world far beyond our present awareness. But right now, dear friend, remember the quest is still the greatest adventure of all. God bless you on your journey.

Rosemary Fillmore Rhea
Unity Village, Missouri

Preface

Dear *Unity Magazine*: Do you suppose Divine Spirit might guide you to relieve Thomas Shepherd of his duties? I find his answers to readers' letters, more often than I'd like, less than "enlightened"—and I'm sure the magazine's founder, Charles Fillmore, would agree. When it comes to Eastern thought, Shepherd doesn't seem to have a clue what it's all about (and should steer clear of it!) I'm sure you can find a very able replacement!
— **Disgruntled, Yountville, California**

Dear Disgruntled: Ouch. My first impulse was to recite the differences between Mahayana and Theravada Buddhism, then cite a few passages from the Hindu scriptures, but that would have been adolescent. You're absolutely right about Mr. Fillmore. Doubtless, he would have disagreed with some things I've written in this column. But I like to think Charles and I could have a zesty discussion of our differences, after which I would be a much better theologian and Mr. Fillmore would have made lots of notes for a new book.

Like the above exchange, this book represents questions (not always friendly) and answers (not always "correct") drawn from more than 15 years of accumulated letters, notes and e-mails delivered to my Q&A column at *Unity Magazine*.

There is no way all of them could find their way into these pages, but I believe we have reproduced a good sampling. Although *Unity Magazine* is a publication of Unity School of Christianity, I have always tried to respond in inclusive language whenever possible. In that spirit, some of the letters and replies have been edited for the widest possible readership without changing the essential content of either the inquiry or my remarks. For example, several questions which began, *"What does Unity believe about ..."* have been amended to read, *"What do you believe about ..."*

Most of my responses stand as written, although none but the foolish would miss the opportunity to expand on incomplete thoughts or correct ideas which are no longer held. The first six years of this column were written before the beginning of the new millennium and the watershed event of September 11. Consequently, some early replies reflect a naïveté which I was tempted to excise but did not. Other answers came in the heat of the Iraqi invasion, and in some of these comments I sound a bit more militaristic than I would if I were writing today.

Rather than fix everything, I have preferred to fine-tune and supplement, hoping the reader will see, as I struggle to learn and grow, the same kind of process which has motivated theologians throughout the ages. The letters of Paul were answers to questions, as were arguably many passages in the Gospels. (*"You have heard it said ... but I say unto you ..."*) *Myrtle Fillmore's Healing Letters* responded to inquiries from readers, and the same kind of struggle to express coherent, helpful thoughts can be seen in her compassionate answers. Writing a Q&A column is a daunting task, one that is undiminished by the realization that I follow two giants down the sunlit valley—my predecessors in this series were Charles Fillmore and Marcus Bach.

I have also tried to reproduce comments from some of the unhappier questioners. Often their complaints flow from a misunderstanding in something I have said, but every minister knows that there will be people who will listen to your message and decide in their heart of hearts that you are not their friend. (And sometimes they hit the target; I am not always right. Ask my wife.) People are people, and all of us struggle to love and be loved, to provide shelter and comfort for our loved ones, and to make sense out of a confusing and sometimes senseless world. I can honestly say that I bear no ill feelings toward anyone today and am eager to continue making whatever meager contribution I can to the great work of establishing world peace and moving toward a global society which can journey as one people to the stars.

The late poet laureate of *Unity Magazine* and longtime Fillmore co-worker, James Dillet Freeman, wrote that Charles sometimes interrupted students *when they were quoting him* and demanded them to think through the question and arrive at their answer.[1] To me, that give-and-take dialogue is the essence of the message of Jesus, who seems to have believed that people must find God for themselves. Jesus practiced creative engagement through an ongoing conversation with the religious thinkers of his day—Pharisees, Sadducees, scribes and teachers of the law. I'd like to think some of them were persuaded to rethink their belief systems and personal ethics by the issues he raised. And who knows—Jesus may have learned something from them too. We don't have to agree on everything, but to live and thrive in a 21st-century, postmodern world with its multiple cultures, economic interdependence and instant communications, surely we must agree on the principle of ongoing, reflective dialogue. So I invite your critique for edification and corrective adjustment. However, I won't stop writing about Eastern thought, especially the Near Eastern mystical prophet Jesus of Nazareth.

I confess to a hidden agenda in all these columns, which is to convince spiritually minded people about the value of critical reflection and to help them think theologically about their lives, relationships and the Divine within. Heart and head must work together, for disparaging either will condemn humanity to fanaticism or ignorance. God will be with us every step of the way—this I passionately believe. Good questions, relentless seeking after truth, and continuous rethinking of the Christian faith throughout the ages to come can bring us closer to reaching through our primitive notions about life in the heavenly clouds of paradise and take us to heights undreamed as the human race continues to grow both intellectually and spiritually.

Blessings on your journey.

"Theology begins with wonder

and unanswered questions."

— Avery Cardinal Dulles, S.J.

Introduction

Many folks whom I have encountered in more than 30 years of ministry are spiritual refugees, thinking and caring people who have nevertheless been driven from the churches of their youth by practices which border on child abuse. If you have any doubt about the mental cruelty of some religionists toward their young people, see the documentary movie *Jesus Camp*. I hear the tears in their words, feel the emptiness and disappointment they experienced in other churches, and try to respond with understanding and compassion.

In this endeavor I must listen carefully to what hurting people say, because I had nothing but good experiences in the mainline church of my childhood, and it is important to me that I do not lose that perspective. Like many other people I was not *driven* out of an oppressive church; I *migrated* from a healthy church background because I suspected there was more to the story. It was nothing like a classical fairy tale, fleeing into a dark and stormy night to avoid the murderous clutches of a jealous stepmother. My coming of age was more like leaving a good home to seek your fortune.

In my earliest memory of the Church, I am a toddler standing in a shaft of light at a low table in the Sunday school of Zion's Evangelical and Reformed Church. Zion's was formerly a German-American house of worship, and its mixed ethnic congregation of the 21st century still meets at the old stone building at the corner of Cedar and Washington Streets in Reading, Pennsylvania. In my memory, I look up from a coloring book of Bible stories and see glowing colored glass and feel the warmth of the sun on my face. A lady places a plate of oval, buttery Keebler Townhouse crackers on the table. She smiles, because I am the reason they serve Townhouse. A few weeks ago, somebody had brought a box, and I had liked them. Zion's was that kind of church. No threats of hell; no exhortations to repent and be saved. Just Townhouse crackers to munch and Bible stories to color. *Be a good boy, tell the truth, treat people with respect, because Jesus loves everyone.* I remember coloring the page where Jacob wrestles all night with the angel to win his blessing. Yet I never felt like God needed that kind of rowdy encouragement to bless me, because the adults around me assumed, "God is great, God is good, all the time."

Oh, sure. There were pesky lines in the liturgy about how "we have grievously sinned against Thee in thought, word, and deed ..." But during every church service, the Rev. Harry Keim, the white-haired, grandfatherly minister, read the "Assurance of Pardon," which promised "the comforting assurance of the grace of God, as promised in the Gospel, to all who repent and believe ..."[1] Then Rev. Keim announced that everyone was forgiven, and that settled it. He shook their hands at the door and never spoke of it again. Until next week, when the process repeated.

Introduction

Old memories are hard to focus sharply, but I recall his sermons were a disaster. I loved the wizened old man, who had been born in the 1890s, but sometimes Rev. Keim lost track of what he was saying. He wandered, mumbled, blew his nose into a white hanky. He never said a word I remember today, even after suffering through years of his worship services and an intensive period of small-group study with Rev. Keim to learn the *Heidelberg Catechism*. As a rite of passage in the German Reformed tradition, the Catechism was a boring, soporific gateway through which all young people must pass in order to officially join the church. We were supposed to memorize huge chunks of its Q&A text, but I cannot believe anyone in his right mind would expect a middle schooler to learn all 128 exchanges, which stretched out like a freight train, or a string of German nouns, with some individual answers running several printed pages. I only learned part of the first line, but I still recall it today:

> Q: What is thy only comfort in life and death?
> A: That I with body and soul, both in life and death, am not my own, but belong unto my faithful Savior Jesus Christ ...[2]

Could young people have a good discussion about that? Sure! In fact, I had plenty of questions, but asking the minister was like Moses trying to reason with the Burning Bush—*Take off your shoes and pay attention; you're here to listen.* To an impatient boy like me, Harry Keim seemed incongruent, confusing and pretty much incapable of explaining anything logically. I came away a new church member without a clue about what depths Christianity had to offer a young, inquisitive mind.

Shaking hands with Rev. Keim, however, was itself a mystical-metaphysical experience. Here was a bona fide man of God. He embraced the divine so frequently in his devotional life that you could smell God's breath on his lapels. His hands were velvety soft, pink and fleshy, and always warm to the touch. I remember looking up at him fondly, wondering if this white-haired old man was God Himself. He was old enough for the job. It sure felt like I was standing in the Divine Presence whenever I was near him. Harry Keim was a pastoral presence, a deep spiritual wellspring from which we dipped pure water of the Gospel, without any need to understand. Did Moses really want to trade the radiant glory of YHWH's presence for the clarity of a talk show host?

Harry Keim was about heart and love. He had tons of both.

When he retired, soon after I became a teenager, Zion's United Church of Christ entertained a new candidate for his post, a recent graduate of Lancaster Theological Seminary, the Reverend G. Richard Ott. And believe me, Rev. Ott was the mirror opposite of Harry Keim. Young, thin, logical and intellectually engaging. The congregation observed his worship leadership one Sunday and then voted on whether to call him to Rev. Keim's vacant pulpit. There was only one *no* vote. Do you have to guess who? Although it was a secret ballot, my grandmother was certain everybody knew I was the only naysayer, and she cried all the way home from church. It was the only time in my otherwise happy youth when I considered running away from home.

Richard Ott came bouncing into Zion's and brought with him youthful energy and a bag of new ideas. It was the early 1960s, and civil rights were a main point in discussion. Rev. Ott spoke, carefully but forcefully, about God as the Lord of all people and said all people are equal because we are one in Christ. He spoke about current events, suggested new inter-pretations of Scripture, and enjoyed raising controversial points occasionally.

One day I was standing outside his office, which was not much more than a closet, on the first floor off the narthex, and he said something that altered my world forever. I was telling him that I found Judaism appealing because I had trouble believing in the divinity of Jesus. At first he tried to give me permission to think freely by telling me that I didn't have to believe in the virgin birth to be a Christian. But that wasn't the world-shaking comment. The life-changing moment came when he spoke rather casually about his own education for the ministry.

Here's my best recollection of what he said. "I was going to attend another seminary, but then I realized that all their graduates sounded like they were stamped out of the same mold. So I went to Lancaster, because I wanted to go some-place where we could wrestle with the theological issues."

Wrestle with the theological issues ... like Jacob wrestling with the angel?

At which sound the heavens opened, and a Great Voice saith unto me, *"Yes, dummy—there are theological issues, and it's okay to wrestle with them ... yea, verily, it's what you're supposed to do!"*

All my young life, I had thought you went to church to *get* a religion. This gave me but two choices, accept or reject. Tell me what we believe, and I'll see if it fits in my world. Rev. Ott had opened a new door—you don't have to suck it all down like a nursing infant. Adults get to look at the menu and find what works for them. And you can even go into the kitchen and discuss the ingredients with the chef, or cook something up yourself. In that offhanded remark, I was reborn. My life as a theologian had begun. I could now go forth and wrestle with the angels myself.

It was only a matter of time before I realize how perfectly my first two ministers had complemented each other. Harry Keim was the feeling nature, and Richard Ott balanced the picture with his bright intellect and hunger for God with his mind. When you bring these together, the result is theological reflection grounded in a circle of faith. *Behold, I have made all things new ...*

Introduction

Method and Content

Recently, I read a remarkable exchange of letters (from the Archives at Unity Institute) between Myrtle Page and Charles Fillmore that echoes this dual nature of the spiritual life. They contain a remark which sounds like a game-changer too. Unity began as a healing movement which employed the tools of theology to examine its concepts.[3] The historical record shows that Unity's founders reveled in theological dialogue about their spiritual goals. One letter to Charles, dated September 1, 1878, contains the following eyebrow-raised retort from the future Mrs. Fillmore:

> You question my orthodoxy? Well, if I were called upon to write out my creed it would be rather a strange mixture. I am decidedly eclectic in my theology—is it not my right to be? Over all is a grand idea of God, but full of love and mercy.[4]

It is okay to be "decidedly eclectic in my theology" as long as it is grounded in a "grand idea of God ... full of love and mercy." Wowzers. I wonder if Charles ever questioned her orthodoxy again.

Like my two predecessors in this column, Charles Fillmore and Marcus Bach, when sketching answers to questions raised by readers, I have attempted to offer grand ideas that are full of love and mercy and deeply eclectic in theology. The process of spiritual inquiry requires an understanding of theological reflection.

Theology has two primary meanings, depending on whether one is speaking about *method* or *content*. As method, theology refers to the study of religious thought; however, theology can also mean the content of a belief system. Students can speak of Roman Catholic theology, and they can do a theological analysis of its specific teachings, like the Catholic ban on birth control. Any "ology" word has this kind of dual standing. A scientist speaks of the biology of the Galapagos Islands, meaning the specific kinds of plants and animals to be found, while the same scientist uses biological procedures to investigate the flora and fauna of those islands.

Let me reiterate: theology as method is analysis of religious values and beliefs; it is not any particular set of beliefs. When scholars speak of the theology of Martin Luther King Jr., they are talking about the way King understood God, life, eternity, the Bible and everything which shaped his spiritual thinking. When seminary professors teach theology, they can teach it as a series of beliefs or as a process of analyzing a belief system. I suggest the best of all worlds is a judicious look at both method and content. In this book, we'll be doing just that.

The Unity Quadrilateral: Thinking Theologically

But before we explore these letters and my fumbling attempts to reply, I also think it's a good time to look at a methodology borrowed from the Methodists themselves, the Wesleyan Quadrilateral, named after the father of

Introduction

Methodism, John Wesley. In several of my books and in my classes here at Unity Institute, I have introduced this simple, effective tool, which provides an easy-to-use formula to establish dialogue among four sources of theology: *Scripture, Tradition, Experience* and *Reason*.[5]

More recently, I've been promoting the idea of a *Unity Quadrilateral*: Scripture, Tradition, Experience and *Reflection*, the latter category divided into intuitive insight and intellectual analysis. Think of the Quadrilateral as a way of processing any religious or spiritual idea. Simply feed the concept into this handy theologizing machine and see what kind of insights you can achieve with your head and heart.

1) Scripture—What did the authors of the foundational documents of the faith say to their target audiences, and what does that mean today?

2) Tradition—What have others thought about this, and how has it been incorporated into the life of the Church?

3) Experience—What have the events of my life and relationships taught me about this; what has science (including the social sciences) taught me about the world?

4) Reflection—In my earlier books, I invoked the historic wording of the Quadrilateral (scripture, tradition, experience and *reason*). Now I am persuaded the last category is better expressed by the word *reflection*, rather than reason. Theological thinking has a dual dimension, *intellectual* and *intuitive/inspirational*. *Intellectual reasoning* asks what sense

can I make of this by thinking it through logically and requiring it to remain consistent with other knowledge? *Intuitive reflection* seeks imaginative insights as I let these ideas play in my mind.

The Unity Quadrilateral is especially helpful when interpreting the Judeo-Christian Scripture. Although it's ancient literature, judging from my letter traffic the Bible is still a major concern to readers in the 21st century. Assuming the biblical documents contain a wealth of wisdom and Truth—a reasonable deduction when considering its positive influence through the centuries—one must nevertheless decide how to interpret Scripture to enable people to access its treasures today. The first factor which comes into play when reading the Bible is the *Scripture* itself—the plain sense of the text. To whom was it written, and for what purposes? Next is the whole history of how people have read and understood the passage, including various "metaphysical" explanations of the text as allegories about soul growth (*tradition*). People also bring personal, cultural and societal *experience* to the reading of the Bible. Finally, humans apply their power to *reflect* both critically and creatively, which includes intellectual thought and creative visioning.

This fourfold process can help with more than just biblical texts. One can use *Scripture-Tradition-Experience-Reflection* when mulling over any religious, sociopolitical, interpersonal or ethical concern. The Unity Quadrilateral is a great tool for thinking theologically about matters metaphysical.

Introduction

From the beginning of their life work, the Fillmores wanted Unity to provide affirmative prayer support, spiritual publications and adult education for the world. With almost an evangelistic fervor, Charles Fillmore announced in January 1906 that his "guidance" from God was to share spiritual truth with everyone:

> The Spirit told us nearly 20 years ago that we should establish here [in the Kansas City area] a great spiritual centre that would radiate its power to all parts of the world, and that people every-where would feel its life-warmth as universally as they do the sun.[6]

The insights of Scripture and traditional interpretations of biblical themes, tempered by communal and individual experience and filtered through the lens of intellectual and intuitive reflection, provide the foundation on which metaphysical Christianity's distinctive blend of Eastern and Western thought continues to unfold. Theology begins when people process incoming ideas through resources like the Unity Quadrilateral and ask critical questions of their own beliefs in the light of the received critique. After this internal dialogue has done its work, it will be possible to respond with alternative ideas, which may even incorporate some of the views of the other person. The result can be mutually beneficial dialogue, which may include complete disagreement on all points. Even agreeing to disagree, as it is popularly called, will strengthen everyone involved if the process of agreeable disagreement proceeds with collegial respect.

In this spirit, which reflects nothing less than the hope of all humanity for a world governed by peace and justice and grounded in the love of God and neighbor, I am remembering the contributions of ordinary saints, like Harry Keim and G. Richard Ott; acknowledging the great work done by the founders of metaphysical Christianity; and celebrating the truth which can doubtless be found in all the religious traditions of humanity. Now let's proceed to look at some really *Good Questions*.

And if you'll agree to wrestle with the angels, I'll try hard not to sound like the *Heidelberg Catechism*.

-1-

Letters From the Edge of Doubt

Dear Tom: Your column has really made me look closely at some negative feelings I've had about Jesus Christ. Raised in a highly traditional church, I rejected veneration of Jesus and studied other faiths. I have come to honor Jesus as a Way Shower, my Way Shower. Your thought-provoking columns are extremely helpful to this seeker. You bring knowledge, critical thinking and the courage to make tough statements. I especially like the fact that you make no attempt to appear infallible.
— **P.M., Oroville, California**

Dear P.M.: No way could I get away with infallibility; I am a married man. But thanks for your kind words. Critical thinking doesn't mean "criticizing your opponents." It means thinking clearly, asking good questions, and requiring every idea to pay its own way rather than grant it free access because it comes to us from some sort of authority. I also like your position on Jesus, as best I understand it from your brief letter. *Way Shower* sounds right to me, because it describes historically and theologically what Jesus has done for the people who have walked his path. We follow Jesus because he knows the path.

Let me add one more point, which is a blind spot for a lot of progressive-thinking people today: Many of us have isolated ourselves from the great new reformation taking place in mainline Protestant and mystical Catholic thinking, to the mutual impoverishment of all players. Spiritual seekers have so many friends in high places, so many allies and fellow seekers on the journey to Christ consciousness, that I would encourage you not just to explore writers you know but to look beyond to spiritual soul mates in the mainstream church. Take a look at outstanding books like *Honest to Jesus* by Robert Funk, *The Heart of Christianity* by Marcus Borg, *Rescuing the Bible From Fundamentalism* by former Episcopal bishop John Shelby Spong, and *Remedial Christianity* by Paul Laughlin.

We are not alone in the night. The bright future of progressive Christianity cannot, must not, be constrained by a self-imposed, self-righteous isolation from those who stand near to us in the family of Jesus Christ. And then, as members of that kinship in the Christ, we can reach confidently beyond the circle of Christian faith to the wider family of humanity to explore more Truth and savor the unknown gospels of other traditions.

Dear Tom: I find myself questioning some things that have been ingrained in me from birth. I grew up in a strict Christian home. I cannot turn my back on some of the beliefs that were instilled in me early on. However, I feel that there has to be more, and I want to learn all that I can. How can I know what the right place is for me?

— **J.P., Jackson, Mississippi**

Dear J.P.: There is no need to turn your back on lifelong beliefs. If they work for you, they're right for you. My friend, the traveling Buddhist monk Bhante Wimala, says his goal is to help Christians become better Christians. Love and wisdom are the best guides. Go within and seek your guidance, then go boldly where your heart takes you, as long as your head can support the journey.

Dear Tom: Why do you think that God is confined in one religion?

— **S.I., via Internet**

Dear S.I.: Oh, I don't. In fact, one could argue that God reveals Him-/Her-/Itself in differing ways, depending on the needs of the believer. What grows in the desert may not transplant to the seashore; your path up the mountain may take you far astray of my tack. God is the One, but we experience ourselves as many. It's perfectly logical that different kinds of cultures will produce different religions. As I tell my students at Unity Institute, *there are no tiger gods where there are no tigers.* Listen for the divine roar, and see what symbol of the One Power and One Presence calls to you.

Dear Tom: The Law of Mind Action seems to be an example of the principle of cause and effect. A simple rendering of cause and effect is an example of a Newtonian or mechanical worldview. Given our contemporary understanding of a dynamic, multifocal quantum perspective, what are the implications for the idea that any effect can be simplistically traced back to a given cause?
— **S.B., San Francisco, California**

Dear S.B.: You are raising a complex and controversial issue, one that I've written about before—whether the spiritual practices are better understood as immutable divine law or as *principles and tendencies*. Because this complex question keeps occurring, I'd like to answer it more completely, starting with some historical background.

Classical civilizations believed the divine powers caused natural phenomena and virtually every event in life. God, or the gods, sent rain and sunshine depending on their inscrutable divine will. Then Sir Isaac Newton (1642–1727) broke the supernatural model of nature by declaring that everything in the world could be understood as math and mechanics. "The latest authors, like the most ancient, strove to subordinate the phenomena of nature to the laws of mathematics," he wrote. "God created everything by number, weight and measure."[1]

Everything was quantifiable, and that which could be counted, weighed and measured could be reliably depended upon to act in predictable ways. Newton's elegant system reduced the whims of the gods to absolute, immutable scientific laws. No longer did humans need to imagine God cranking up the sunrise or spreading stars across the sky at night. Newton showed the science behind the curtain of reality. And Newtonian physics has worked with mathematical precision, or NASA wouldn't be able to shoot rockets to Mars and beyond with faultless accuracy.

However, by the early 20th century, science began to realize that when looking deep into the subatomic level, the elegant, cause-and-effect mechanical model of Isaac Newton just ain't necessarily so. The fact is that current scientific theory speaks less about laws and more about *aggregate tendencies and probabilities*, less about matter and energy and more about matter-energy events. The physics behind this new quantum paradigm is at once far too complex and counterintuitive to explain here, although a good primer is the popular movie *What the Bleep!? Down the Rabbit Hole.*

However, to help you understand the new model, I offer you this behavioral example: Think about a college football game. If the home team scores a touchdown, we can predict with 100 percent accuracy that the stadium will erupt with cheers. However, we can predict less accurately what will happen in seat D-321. Perhaps the seat will be empty or the person in seat D-321 will be from out of town and rooting for the visiting team or will have personal problems which distract him or her from celebrating. In the aggregate, we have some degree of certainty. Individually, we have only probabilities and tendencies. The same is apparently true with subatomic particles. In the aggregate, science can predict what will happen to billions of atoms with astonishing accuracy, but the behavior of an individual subatomic particle is not so predictable. Science today speaks less of immutable laws and more in terms of probabilities and tendencies.

If we apply this quantum understanding to spiritual practices, it becomes readily apparent why sometimes we get results and other times we don't. If we consider that God works through cause and effect—do this and that must happen—then we are indeed operating out of a Newtonian worldview. However, if we recognize that there is this pesky quantum thingy operating, we begin to wonder whether the subatomic particles themselves have a measure of free will. Maybe there's a random factor programmed into the mix, something to keep us moving, mystified, evolving and learning. Perhaps there's something to test our resolve and make us try again, and again, and again—if necessary. Maybe there's something to build our faith that, regardless of appearances to the contrary, God is good, life is good, and God has everything under control.

It seems to me that the important factor in spiritual life isn't controlling the outcome or demonstrating this or that. Some Buddhists believe the most important element in spirituality is detachment, so that whatever happens, one can stay centered and accept it with gracious dignity and strong faith. Faith in God really isn't about controlling power or immutable laws; it's about employing the divine principles with love and entrusting the outcome to God. When confronted with a circumstance in which you would like to be healed, prospered or filled with joyful success, there are age-old spiritual principles to draw upon. The law of mind action is one of them: *Thoughts held in mind produce after their kind*. In this westernized version of karma, you get back what you send out. However, I would modify the above with the addition of your "dynamic, multifocal quantum perspective" and a Buddhist postscript: You tend to get back what you send out, but whatever happens, stay centered and be at peace.

Dear Tom: Astronomers estimate that the Milky Way galaxy has 300 billion stars and that there are at least 100 billion other galaxies. Astronomers also estimate that the universe is about 13 billion years old. Did God create all that? If not, how did it come into existence?

— D.J.P., Iowa City, Iowa

Dear D.J.P.: Cosmology is a bit above my pay grade, but I find one answer to the riddle of existence in the tiger lily, the lovely, trumpet-shaped, speckled orange flower which greets me along the road to Unity Village every summer day. But hold that thought for a moment. Yes, the cosmos is a mighty big place, but whether it was created or has always existed is still an open question. The fundamental pattern of the universe could be linear (beginning to end) or cyclical (repeating), although the latter would require some kind of renewal once in a while (every few dozen billion years) when the laws of entropy run their course and all energy burns itself out. Would that constitute a new creation?

Anyway, this is heady stuff to contemplate, and although I am flattered when asked to explain how the universe came to be, you probably should consult a higher Authority. You may discover the heart of the universe is not so difficult to fathom after all. I don't need astrophysics to appreciate tiger lilies. I have no idea whether someone planted them or if they just sprang from the weeds by an act of natural selection. But they sure are pretty, and that's good enough for me.

Dear Tom: How about religion versus spirituality? Where, if at all, do the two interconnect? And what is the difference between them? Or, more succinctly, can one be spiritual without a belief in an omnipotent God?
— S.T., Naperville, Illinois

Dear S.T.: Religion can best be described as a community of faith distinguished by a generally held system of beliefs and practices that are advocated by a recognizable body of believers. In other words, identifying a person's religion is like discovering his or her language and ethnic background. It merely gives us common ground, a place to start, as it is impossible to know what particular beliefs a person who claims to be a Jew or Muslim or Christian might espouse. There are even atheistic Christians—that may seem odd, but it's true! The whole "God is dead" movement years ago came from that radical wing of the church, especially through the writings of Thomas J. J. Altizer. Although Christian atheism has never won popular support, in the years since the "death of God" controversy, academic theology has drifted toward a denial of the classical God concept, in favor of a broader definition of the Divine. In fact, mainstream Christian thought is moving steadily toward a position not unlike the views often expressed by mystics through the ages, some of whom held that there is an underlying Oneness to all things, and that God can best be understood as the One Presence and One Power causing everything to exist.

So I would have to answer *yes*, it is possible to be "spiritual" without the belief in an omnipotent God. Buddhists generally hold that nontheistic position, and the traditional view of God sitting on a throne no longer works for many people in the West as well. However, I can't help wondering how it's possible to be "spiritual" without belief in the Divine *Spirit* that permeates all things and causes the cosmos to be.

Dear Tom: I find myself more and more drawn toward a universal spirituality that goes beyond any particular religion. Maybe it's because I can't identify with the basic doctrines of Christianity anymore, or maybe it's because I am rather impatient with fundamentalism of any kind. I like the teachings of Jesus, but I'm having difficulty calling myself a Christian because I can't affirm beliefs like the virgin birth, blood atonement, the Second Coming or the infallibility of the Bible. How does a thinking person, who wants to be spiritually and

intellectually honest, call himself a Christian in the 21st century?
— **C.C., Honolulu, Hawaii**

Dear C.C.: Yes, it is a challenge to balance heart and head, but that is probably true in every religion. All faiths have their mythological elements that, taken literally, impose an ordeal upon thoughtful believers. I have attended three Protestant seminaries, and I found no one—faculty, staff or student— who believed in a strictly literal interpretation of the Bible. The task for modern disciples of the great gurus of antiquity is to shake free from the limitations imposed by any ancient worldview in order to soar to the heights glimpsed by those master teachers of humanity. I find Jesus reacting exactly this way to the fundamentalists of his day.

Progressive Christianity today recognizes the strong current of truth flowing deeply through all the religious traditions of humanity. But it's also good to have a home base, a religio-cultural context, a spiritual worldview with which to identify. We don't have to abandon our distinctive Judeo-Christian cultural and religious heritage in order to affirm the oneness of humanity and the basic truth of all religions, any more than we have to become citizens of China to enjoy steamed rice and egg rolls. At its highest expression, Christianity is inclusive, not exclusive. Don't let the fundamentalists define the terms for you.

I recently hosted a series of classes taught by the venerable Bhante Wimala, who describes himself a "traveling Buddhist monk." I was impressed by many things about Bhante, but most of all by the fact that his high degree of commitment to

Buddhism doesn't make him even slightly ethnocentric about his religious faith. He speaks and lives as a Buddhist, but he acts like a citizen of the world. I highly recommend Bhante Wimala's book *Lessons of the Lotus*. Bhante offers a modern version of the affirming, cross-cultural love displayed by Jesus of Nazareth, who met with outcasts, sinners and all sorts of gentiles—even the much-despised Romans. Jesus was a Jew, but, like Bhante's Buddhism, his religion didn't limit him, *it set him free.*

As more neighborhoods of this global village come together, there will be more opportunities for sharing across the back fence, so to speak. Suddenly, the exhortations of Jesus to "love thy neighbor" and "love thine enemies" take on prophetic dimensions. Key phrases from the man of Nazareth fairly leap across the centuries when viewed from the global village: *Blessed are the peacemakers. Go the second mile. Return not evil for evil. Neither do I condemn thee. My house shall be a house of prayer for all nations. A house divided cannot stand.*

A religion should not be defined by manmade doctrines, but by the spirit of love it engenders in the hearts of its followers. If you find yourself inspired by the affirming love of Jesus, if you look to his model as a way of understanding what it means to be human and divine, feel free to call yourself a Christian—or not. Labels, although not unimportant, mean less than the actions they inspire.

Dear Tom: For the first time in human history, democracy is entering into the realm of religion and showing itself as a way of life that includes diversity of faith and the need for mutual respect between the religions of the world, as well as between all aspects of life. This change of consciousness has very powerful implications for the ministry and for the life of Spirit expressing in our society. It calls for a new kind of ministry; one which is not devoted to one religion alone, but rather which seeks harmony between the many paths and an awareness of our universal heritage.

— **L.S., Los Angeles, California**

Dear L.S.: Your ambitions are noble and somewhat lofty; not a few people have tried unsuccessfully to construct a new religion from shards found among the others. The modern version of this is to pronounce oneself "interfaith" and eschew all denominational labels. One problem with this kind of militant syncretism is the table of religious dialogue has no designated *interfaith* seat. The table may be interfaith, but all the chairs are marked *Buddhist, Muslim, Baha'i, Hindu* and so on. Paradoxically, a self-proclaimed "interfaith" ministry is not the voice of a wider religious community but merely speaks for those few people who have gathered under the strength of one minister's charisma. Instead of representing all faiths, the "interfaith" ministry actually fences its congregation into a denomination of one.

If you are seeking an expression of personal beliefs, that is, a religious philosophy utterly detached from all other persons, an independent interfaith ministry is the way to go. However, what I hear people hungering for is not an uncommitted, abstract philosophy but a workable *theology*, which begins within a circle of generally shared beliefs and practices. Properly understood, theology is not a system of required beliefs and practices; theology is an ongoing *discussion* about beliefs and practices with shared starting points which can lead to deeper spiritual insight and experience.

I would argue that holding one set of beliefs need not require complete rejection of all other possibilities; religions need not be mutually exclusive. While it is possible to journey alone on your spiritual quest—like a fish can be alone in a fishbowl—the social sciences and supportive historical studies show that authentic spiritual life tends to flow best from the experiences of a community which shares some combined sense of history and destiny. I approach the interfaith table as an open-minded subscriber to the Judeo-Christian worldview. I suggest a descriptive term for this is to call oneself "culturally Christian, spiritually unlimited."

Dear Tom: Why should I call myself a Christian, when I find truth in all the great religions? Why live in the past, when all we have is now?
— T.M.Y., Atlanta, Georgia

Dear T.M.Y.: I hear from people all the time who want to move beyond labels into something fresh and new. There is also a strong movement about living in "the Now" as opposed to living in the past or future. This is a grand idea, but living in "the Now" is greatly overrated in popular literature today. Of course, all one ever has is "now" because time moves onward. And some events of the past must be shaken away before they crash the programs for today and tomorrow. Like the running back in American football who gets sacked behind the line of scrimmage, people who continue to dwell on the failures of the past will not have their mind in the game and the next play will likely be a fumble or a worse loss of yardage.

When I played school football, a long lifetime ago, the coach always told us to shake off the current play and get our heads back in the game, *now!* But that hardly means the coach had no plan for the future and no memory of the mistakes we made which needed to be corrected by supplemental training next week. It's not *all* about now, as most of "the Now" literature quietly admits.

No one moves into the future without coming from the present, which is predicated by a whole lot of events in the past. Let's test this theory. Look out the window. Stop reading, go to the window—I'm serious. I'll wait right here ...

Back already?

What did you see? Whatever it was, I am confident as I sit here in Lee's Summit, Missouri, that you looked out at the same world I did. (Well, okay. If this book of snappy replies becomes a deathless classic, you might be reading a few centuries in the future and looking up from a ringed planet with a dozen moons. Same idea works ... you'll see.)

My point is, you looked out at a world which you did not consciously create but inherited at birth. That world has shaped your thinking in ways most people never consider. How different would your worldview be if you saw minarets and domed mosques in the distance? What it were spiked

Buddhist temples, gothic cathedrals or a Shinto gate—how would life in the societies which produced such structures affect your values? What if you saw no prominent religious buildings but just a city skyline or mountains carpeted with pine trees or desert expanses or ocean beaches stretching in the distance? Would that mean you are free from the world-views, religious traditions and systems of valuation which have come from the past?

You are inexorably, organically, evolutionarily invested in a time and place, language and intellectual processes, history and culture and value system—all of which you inherited from others.

Even if you have utterly rejected the living religions, dominant philosophies or current political theories of your cultural heritage, you have likely paid indirect homage to those ideas by forming a counterreformation against those earlier images and values. Rejection is shaped by that which it rejects. Few atheists today actively campaign against an Old Nordic belief system based on Thor and Odin, but instead target the *Jehovah-in-the-Sky* of classical Christian theism. Postmodern scientists are disinclined to write papers denouncing the flat-earth theory; politicians no longer argue about the gold standard; philosophers seldom revisit the anti-slavery debates of the 19th century because the abolition of slavery has now become a global norm.

The world people inherit powerfully affects the way they see that world, but there are other options. The hidden, sub-versive—nay, verily, *evangelical*—goal of this volume is to awaken readers to their embedded theologies, to equip 21st-century people with better tools to understand themselves in this emerging, pluralistic, global society. For those of us standing in shallows of the great stream of tradition founded by Jesus Christ, I call this open state of mind "culturally Christian, spiritually unlimited," as I mentioned in a previous letter. The formula works in any context: culturally Muslim, Jewish, Buddhist, Hindu, Taoist, Nativistic, *etc.*, spiritually unlimited. It is this marriage of neotraditional identity with postmodern openness to many truths which can allow a genuine interfaith community to develop. Not as a new amalgamation of practices and beliefs picked from the buffet table of religious thought and practice, but an interfaith Christianity, interfaith Islam, interfaith Judaism, interfaith Hinduism—continue the list with any religious tradition. *That* kind of interfaith movement has the potential to unite the world.

-2-

Theodicy: The Primordial Question

(If God Is Good, Why Do Bad Things Happen?)

Dear Tom: How can people like you so confidently believe that God is Absolute Good when so much suffering and evil exist in the world? Would a good God allow children to die from horrible diseases; where was God when the Nazis gassed six million Jews?

— **K.M., New Mexico (no city provided)**

Dear K.M.: You've asked the toughest and most frequently recurring question in religious thought: How to explain "evil" if God is 1) all powerful and 2) all good? Historically, the argument has looked like this: If God *cannot* prevent bad things from happening, then God is not all powerful. And if God *will not* prevent evil, God is not all good.

The problem is known as *theodicy,* and theologians have traditionally offered three types of solutions to the two horns of this dilemma:

1) *God is not all powerful.* God is limited in some ways, and there are some things He/She/It cannot do in an orderly universe.

35

2) *Evil is good for you.* Bad things are not truly evil but a disguised form of good. For example, suffering can be a challenge to faith, a hidden growth experience, a spiritual test.

3) *Evil and suffering are a mystery.* These matters cannot be understood by limited human minds. Resolution to the problem of theodicy will wait until we receive what Catholics call the *beatific vision* in the afterlife.

None of these explanations are very satisfactory, especially for a parent who has just lost a child or any innocent bystander who has suffered the collateral damage which goes with living in a physical universe. Rabbi Harold Kushner's best-selling book *When Bad Things Happen to Good People* makes the following comment, which is the key to the problem:

> All the responses to tragedy which we have considered have at least one thing in common. They all assume that God is the cause of our suffering, and they try to understand why God would want us to suffer. ... We were left either hating ourselves for deserving such a fate or hating God for sending it to us when we did not deserve it. There may be another approach. Maybe God does not cause our suffering.[1]

The confusion begins with a misunderstanding of God's nature. Instead of pulling strings like a puppeteer, perhaps God is not separate from the cosmos. What if God's power in fact animates the very atoms of the universe, yet even the smallest molecule has a measure of free will? Suppose God wants all sentient beings to be happy, healthy and wise and has provided a cosmos in which individualized expressions of Divine Intelligence—you and I—must discover and apply the physical and spiritual principles necessary to produce such happiness, health and wisdom.

If people center themselves on the Truth of God's absolute goodness, even in the face of apparent "evil" and unspeakable suffering; if they rely upon God while walking the valley of the shadow—for that is what evil and suffering are in eternity, mere shadows—then no calamity can overwhelm their sense of okay-ness about life, for they know God has issued a guarantee that everything will work out for the good. This does not mean I should glibly dismiss suffering as an "error in consciousness," or feel superior to people who are in pain, or feel guilty when I face a health challenge or some personal tragedy. For reasons known only to God, that's the kind of universe where humanity was born. What other arrangement allows the freedom necessary for spiritual growth?

Dear Tom: I will answer the perennial question: "Why do bad things happen to good people?" Perhaps a certain plan exists for the whole cosmos in which human beings play only a minor role. Surely all the catastrophes on earth (earthquakes, hurricanes and so forth), where thousands are killed, are not for us to understand. Perhaps humankind is not yet able to understand this and the true nature of God. Surely, God is something greater, almighty, with all good properties. God is identical with unconditional love and goodness. Anyway, we are not yet able to understand this fully.

— F.G., Basel, Switzerland

Dear F.G.: You have precisely identified the problem raised by this stubborn, recurring question. Your answer falls under the third category mentioned in my response to the previous letter: It is a mystery. People find ourselves confronted with a world—which they did not create—in which people both suffer and are blessed unaccountably. All our systems of theology crumble under the weight of this contradiction. Lacking a strong, clear solution to the age-old problem, humans in all religions have generally come to the same conclusion which you did. However, I like the spin on the word *mystery* which comes from reading James Dillet Freeman: While life may be mysterious, it is certainly a wonder. The proper response to wondrous events is not endless analysis but mystical communion with their Source.

Dear Tom: All four of my brothers have myotonic dystrophy, a type of dystrophy that strikes in your mid-30s. I often thank God that I do not have this disease. My question is, How can I thank God for my health without blaming God for the pain and difficulties my brothers must deal with?

— E.M., New Paltz, New York

Theodicy: The Primordial Question

Dear E.M.: That's a tough one. Does God act capriciously, sparing one while spearing another? A common answer across many mystical traditions might startle you: God "sends" neither blessings nor calamities. God has created a cosmos that operates by scientific laws and spiritual principles, and these laws and principles are trustworthy.

Step off a wall, the law of gravity comes into play. The resulting injury has nothing to do with God's lack of kindness. Even a good, saintly person must obey the laws of gravity or suffer the consequences. Babies quickly learn that gravity makes no special provisions for beginners. But gravity also is the positive force holding us safely on the earth and keeping our muscles strong and toned.

Spiritual principles operate similarly, although I often find, unlike Newton's law of gravity, healing doesn't take place instantly. Demonstrating health and prosperity may require some work to out-picture a result. There is some degree of art in the spiritual science of healing, much like a musician improving by steady practice.

The point is that in a cosmos of scientific laws and spiritual principles, the work of humankind is to discover them and use them. People today are starting to see that there are physical, mental and spiritual principles for transforming the ills of humankind and the world. We don't begin to understand them all yet, but it is the work of spiritual growth to learn more about them every day. That's what makes the spiritual quest so rewarding and exciting.

With that starting point, God did not send disease to strike your brothers. They were born into a cosmos in which health challenges can occur (sometimes due to our choices;

sometimes due to randomized genetic or environmental factors), but also one in which health challenges can be healed. Who can doubt that certain spiritual practices will result in better, fuller, richer, healthier, happier, more prosperous lives? You may have heard this before, but it is a truth at the heart of this spiritual universe: What happens to us is not nearly as important as how we respond to it.

Yes, you can give thanks for your own health. Giving thanks is a spiritual principle that promotes health. How important it is, then, to also use that principle in giving thanks for the life of God working in your brothers and for the growing wisdom in them and in humankind to deal with their disease.

When people realize that God has established principles to improve life in this world, they will begin to see how important everyone's part is. The proper response to every circumstance is prayer, trust and openness to new possibilities. Nothing but God is completely trustworthy. As the prophet Isaiah said, "The grass withers, the flower fades; but the word of our God will stand forever" (Isaiah 40:8).

When presented with joy or tragedy, the best and most appropriate response is always prayer that centers us in the One Presence and One Power of God, the good and omnipotent, and opens us to those spiritual principles which can bring healing and transformation to our world. Who knows what new answers to the ills of humankind may be discovered tomorrow? God knows.

Dear Tom: How I wish I had your wonderful conviction about the goodness and all-powerful aspects of God! But I cannot understand how a good and all-powerful God could allow such a thing as the Holocaust or the necessity of animals eating other animals in order to survive. Could God not have arranged to feed them in a less savage way?

— **D.M., Boston, Massachusetts**

Dear D.M.: I suppose God could have designed a cosmos in which the freedom to make horrific choices was not present, but what kind of existence would that be? To be able to choose the good, people must also be able to turn away from goodness to "un-goodness," which is called *evil*. If God is within everyone and everything, both nurturing and allowing women and men to be what they are, then God experiences what people experience—the joys and sufferings—and calls humanity up the evolutionary ladder from primordial "slime" to the edge of a civilization that is reaching for the stars.

All sentient beings are examples of freedom in motion. God was in the victims and guards at the death camps; God is within predator and prey.

Dear Tom: I have always wondered why white-collar thieves who actually and meanly steal someone's fortune make it through life without giving back what they stole. Why does God permit that honest, good people suffer total loss of money because of these thieves? I have not lost my faith and hopefully never will, but I feel very betrayed, not listened to, abandoned. God has already put many, many terrible events in our lives and He seems to get going. I feel terrible to say this, but that's how I feel.

— M.S., via Internet

Dear M.S.: Your pondering is more plaintive than theological, and I feel your hurt.[2] The short answer to your question is, God does not "permit" anything, any more than the force of gravity "permits" someone to fall if he steps off a building. God is the process of life, the power of life, the total program of life. Love and lack of it are two ends of the choices people make using their divine-human powers. There is a natural flow to life, and people know they're in the flow when they can greet the twin imposters of "good" and "evil" with equanimity.

The great religious leaders of humanity have shown that a person of faith does not respond to disappointments and painful circumstances by railing at the heavens, "*Why?!*" Rather, trust in God means asking a wholly different question: "What would you have me do, Lord?" I would argue that all major religious teachers—Moses, Buddha, Jesus, Mohammed, Baha'u'llah, pick your favorite—have said the goal of life is *not to control events, but to let good results out-picture through our thoughts and deeds.* We are not called upon to bend the unseen forces of the cosmos to do our will. With apologies to J. K. Rowling and *Harry Potter*, whom I adore—that's *magic*, and no such supernatural power exists. The goal of practical Christianity is to get yourself out of the way and let God—the natural, health-giving, life-affirming program that is running the cosmos—work its everyday miracles through you.

May I suggest that you meditate on one of my favorite texts from the apostle Paul: "Have no anxiety about anything, but in everything by prayer and supplication with thanksgiving let your requests be made known to God. And the peace of God, which passes all understanding, will keep your hearts and your minds in Christ Jesus" (Philippians 4:6-7).

Dear Tom: Do we overcome our enemies by imitating their behavior? I am highly distressed about the world situation. When will we ever learn, and what can one person do in the real world to effect change?
— **J.M., Chicago, Illinois**

Dear J.M.: That's always the question—how does one live the high principles in a world where force often rules the day? Long-ago Roman emperor Marcus Aurelius, an accomplished stoic philosopher, advised people to live a life of wise tolerance.

Begin each day by telling yourself: Today I shall be meeting with interference, ingratitude, insolence, disloyalty, ill-will, and selfishness—all of them due to the offenders' ignorance of what is good or evil. But for my part I have long perceived the nature of good and its nobility, the nature of evil and its meanness, and also the nature of the culprit himself, who is my brother ... therefore none of these things can injure me, for nobody can implicate me in what is degrading.[3]

Marcus Aurelius lived the dilemma of the philosopher-king, a man of wisdom and compassion called upon to wield power in a world often ruled by brute force. Although I appreciate what the emperor was saying, as a student of metaphysical Christianity I would approach the problem a bit differently. Rather than affirming all the negatives he expected to greet every day, like *interference* and *ingratitude*, why not expect positive experiences of *cooperation, gratitude, respect, loyalty, goodwill* and *selflessness*? The stoic sailed high above the fray and refused to be brought down by the animosity or misbehavior of others, and there are times when stoic fortitude is a highly appropriate response to life. However, why expect the worst, when the mind tends to attract to it that which it anticipates?

-3-
Wrestling With God

> Dear Tom: What book would you recommend for a 19-year-old college student—my son—who is uncertain about whether he believes in a God? He is a brilliant student and disdains my metaphysical beliefs, although he does respect them. We are close, and I would like to send him something to facilitate his spiritual journey without being intrusive.
> — **D.B., Lafayette, Louisiana**

Dear D.B.: In this specific instance—college student exploring the dimensions of his universe—I would recommend one of my favorite spiritual books of all time: *Autobiography of a Yogi* by Paramhansa Yogananda, available online and through most commercial bookstores. Your son may not agree with Yogananda's conclusions, nor fully understand the Hinduism, but he will find himself swimming in the ocean of God's presence almost from page one. Not through theological abstractions (which I love), but through the personal experiences of a God-intoxicated young man coming of age in India at the end of the 19th century. In Yogananda, many young seekers find a kindred soul. It is impossible to read this book and not come away with the conviction that divine power permeates all the cosmos. Metaphysical Christianity didn't grow up in the same neighborhood, but Yogananda's world is only a local call away, because God doesn't hide from those who seek guidance.

I suggest you read *Autobiography of a Yogi*, too, and discuss the ideas with your son. Later, to bridge the gap between cultures, you might try my book *Friends in High Places*, also readily available through online booksellers. It deals with the history of Western spirituality.

Dear Tom: Is God a crutch for the weak of heart and mind? Only some of the things which come our way can be changed. Let's face it—there is no escape from reality. We are just one small part of evolution, although I do agree that a universal energy guides us in this process. The key words are understanding and acceptance. We all search for the real and honest Truth. I believe no one knows the truth.

— **H.F., Massillon, Ohio**

Dear H.F.: If, as you say, "no one knows the truth," how did you come to know *that*? Humans *must* begin with a set of assumptions about themselves and their cosmos. These assumptions are not provable or disprovable. They are not chosen. They come prepackaged inside our heads, programmed by the unique interaction of ourselves and the experiences of life. Before we are old enough to count, we've already decided whether life itself is 1) good/supportive or 2) bad/hostile or 3) valueless/indifferent.

Folks who have good interactions with people and circumstances will probably decide that the universe is good. Others, who have been badly mistreated by people or circumstances, are likely to decide that life is an evil place. There have been times in human history when life in general became much more difficult to bear. For an example from Western civilization, take the period from the fall of Rome through the end of the medieval era. Life was quite harsh, consequently viewing the world as an evil place became the dominant theological perspective. Earth was a vale of tears, teeming with devils whose sole task was to pull humanity into eternal damnation. This unhealthy consciousness gripped the Western world until the Renaissance, when people began to suspect that life wasn't as bad as the medieval Church had painted it.

When life leaves people with a confused jumble of mixed messages—some good, some bad, mostly ambivalent—they might decide also life is a crapshoot and nobody is in charge. These folks alone can be true atheists, because they can look at the drunk in the gutter and the Nobel laureate and see no eternal difference, since both their lives are pointless.

I don't hear you doubting the goodness of life but the logic of belief in God. If the idea of a personal god is incomprehensible to you, drop it. Substitute instead the idea of eternal, Absolute Goodness—in your words, the "universal energy" which "guides us in the process." If you really believe that life is good, supportive and salutary, then you *must* believe the very nature of reality itself is good, supportive and salutary. That, friend, is what God is.

Dear Tom: Could you please explain the difference between God and the Son of God? Thank you.
— **D.O., Santa Monica, California**

Dear D.O.: The classical difference between *God* and the *Son of God* is that the generic term *God* refers to the Divine Creative Energy—the Father/Mother Power which begets and sustains the cosmos, whereas the term *Son of God* conveys what some theologians have called a "finite locus" of the Divine—that is, the infinite God focused at a comprehensible site.

If that's too wordy for you, think of the ocean and a drop of sea water. The drop contains the ocean in miniature. It's made of the same chemical combination, the same salty liquid, as its vast parent. By studying the drop, we learn about the qualities of the sea, certainly not in oceanic fullness but in a representative sample. Unity teachers have traditionally explained the relationship between God and the Son of God as the Divine Mind (Father) which conceives of a perfect Idea (Son) and sends it forward into Expression (Spirit). Note the necessity for the third element, Spirit, to complete the equation. In Christian terms, God the Creator sent forth the Christ into the cosmos to birth the Spirit in all sentient beings.

Dear Tom: Do you think the more you have faith, God will answer more quickly?
— G.C., Sacramento, California

Dear G.C.: Absolutely not. Nothing you can do will speed up or slow down God's rate of action. God is always trying to bring about our highest good. The problem isn't with God; it's with us. When we begin to remove the blocks that we have placed to our good, then like a mighty torrent the blessings come rushing into our open spaces. See any book by Catherine Ponder for more details.

Dear Tom: I have three questions: 1) What the heck does "God's will" imply? Though I have read the Bible many times, I cannot embrace the notion that God has a will for me. 2) Why can't I speak in tongues since my "born again" experience over 25 years ago, in a charismatic renewal setting? 3) Is Jesus my Savior? I have no idea. I only know that he is my good friend, whose convictions and example I honor. Am I missing something?
— K.C., Andover, Massachusetts

Dear K.C.: Ordinarily, I try to prune the inquiries down to one basic issue, but you asked three really good ones.

1) God's will is always the same: the highest good in every circumstance. It's up to you to decide what that is. God doesn't provide cheat sheets for the tests of life, my friend.

2) The practice of "speaking in strange tongues," or ecstatic utterance, is found in various religious traditions around the world, not just the tradition of charismatic Christians. Scientific studies suggest that the gift of tongues, technically called *glossolalia*, isn't really a language, because it lacks the organization and structure of rational speech, but a form of nonverbal, ecstatic prayer. Because this practice disconnects cognitive brain functions from the speech apparatus, glossolalia is not unlike chanting a prayer sound or reciting a mantra.

However, ecstatic prayer isn't just for strictly emotional worshipers. Dr. Marcus Bach, my brilliant and gentlemanly predecessor in this column, experienced glossolalia himself on at least one occasion. Although this gift isn't for everyone—I've never sought the experience—nonverbal, euphoric prayer, which is emotionally based yet completely under the control of the participant, can be a highly meaningful encounter with God. Perhaps you can no longer do it because you've moved beyond this form of spiritual expression, but you shouldn't beat up on yourself if this gift no longer works for you.

3) Whenever I hear the line "Jesus is our savior," I always ask myself: "From what, for what, by what?" Certainly not from some imaginary wrath of God. If the Creator of the universe has problems with anger management, we're in serious trouble. Do we really want a petulant deity juggling the galaxies while managing human destiny in eternity?

The one place in Scripture where Jesus was asked point-blank, "Good Teacher, what must I do to inherit eternal life?" (Mark 10, repeated by Matthew and twice by Luke), he responds by saying, essentially, "Be nice." He tells the questioner to follow the moral and ethical standards of the Ten Commandments and treat his neighbor with respect. Jesus does not say, "Believe in me, confess your sins, and you'll avoid your richly merited damnation." That medieval concept would be incomprehensibly foreign to an orthodox Jew, which Jesus remained all the days of his life. In fact, in the oldest version of the exchange (the Gospel of Mark), Jesus turns aside the question with a mild rebuke, "Why do you call me 'good'? No one is good but God alone."

A lot of metaphysical Christians like to call Jesus their Way Shower, because he marked the Godward path for others to follow. When he declared, "No one comes to the Father but by me" (John 14:6), Jesus was not saying, "Believe in me, or burn in hell!" Jesus was stating a simple truth: each person must find God individually. One could argue that John 14:6 really means "If you want to find God, look within you, the way I did." Discover the Father-Mother God by going directly to headquarters.

Dear Tom: I'd like you to say why, in your opinion, God put us here? I am Catholic, 84 years of age and in good health.
— **R.M., Fresh Meadows, New York**

Dear R.M.: Hmmm ... the meaning of life, briefly stated? My answer is one word: *education.* I've always believed we are here to learn how to be fully human, and recently I've begun to see that we are also here to learn how to become fully divine. Great Catholic thinkers, like the medieval mystical theologian Johannes (Meister) Eckhart, have said that humanity has a destiny in oneness with God.

Everything in life teaches the spiritually attuned person something. Failure offers an opportunity for faith; success offers a chance for gratitude. I only see the jumbled strings on the back of God's tapestry; the Master Weaver sees the grand design.

Dear Tom: I have an ongoing internal debate raging. I want to believe in God, but I've never developed a strong belief and am constantly besieged by doubts about whether God exists or whether humankind has just made Him or Her up because we simply can't face our own mortality. I have been a follower of metaphysical Christianity for years, largely because it does not require following a rigid set of doctrines that have no meaning to me personally. I have read the Bible but often don't understand what is there and find it discouraging when it can be interpreted so many ways by so many faiths.

I enjoy your answers; they are always insightful and frequently break new ground for me. How do you keep your faith, and can you recommend any books or practices that might be meaningful for me?

— E.S., New London, Ohio

Dear E.S.: Thanks for your kind comment. I'm always gratified when someone asks a deeply intellectual question with a spiritual basis. Some people believe spirituality is experienced strictly through the feeling nature, especially by meditation and prayer. While I respect that perspective, feeling-centered activities are not the only path to spiritual growth. Prayer and meditation certainly are the foundations of spirituality, but Jesus said we should love God with the *mind* as well as the heart. One of the descriptive names for metaphysical Christianity is *New Thought*, rather than *New Feel*. So let's break new ground and do some theology.

Technically speaking, it sounds like you're an agnostic— someone who doesn't know if there's a god or not—but leaning toward being an atheist. *Good for you!* Atheism is the perfect religion for Christians. One of the earliest complaints against the Church by educated pagans was that the followers of Jesus were atheists; that is, Christians didn't believe in the gods. But if you think about it, everybody is an atheist in some form or another. For example, I'm reasonably certain the current Pope is an avowed atheist about the Norse gods (Thor, Odin, Loki), and the most devout Muslim on pilgrimage to Mecca is a card-carrying atheist about the Roman gods (Jupiter, Saturn, Neptune; you know, all the planetary gods). I'll even be bold enough to guess that the Dalai Lama is an atheist about the Christian Devil.

It's important to be an atheist about mythological gods. And let's get serious about the classical Christian concept of God—the Omnipotent King, a Supernatural Being, separate from creation and ruling the universe from His exalted throne, who judges men and nations by His righteous might. The great neo-orthodox biblical scholar Rudolf Bultmann debunked that God-concept in his 1941 essay on "The New Testament and Mythology."[1] To people who practice progressive Christianity, the God-concept of classical theism is as mythological as Thor's hammer or Jupiter's thunderbolts. Bultmann went as far as to say we need to find the eternal truth wrapped inside the Bible's prescientific worldview. He called the process "de-mythologizing," and although the essay was a bombshell, Bultmann's views are not even controversial in mainline biblical studies today.

Most atheists are disbelievers in this God-the-Ruler-and-Judge deity, and to them goes my sympathy. God as king and judge, a supernatural being separate from his cosmos, is dualistic. There is God; and there is humanity. A chasm separates, never to be bridged. Even if classical Christian theology suggests the sacrificial death of Jesus can bridge the gap, humans still arrive on the God-side as creatures separate from Creator. It's a better image than sin and alienation, but the reconciliation obtained through traditional Christian salvation schemes is eternally incomplete. The Creator and the creatures remain qualitatively mismatched. He is divine; we are not. Dualism endureth forever.

Another more mystical understanding of the Christian message sees Ultimate Reality as *monistic*, not dualistic. God and creatures are not separate, because God does not "exist" the way other things exist. God is not a mere character in the drama of life, but the paper and pen and ideas and story and words. To explain better, let me introduce you to one of our friends in high places, theologian Paul Tillich (1886–1965). Tillich held that God is not a being but *being* itself, that God does not "exist" the way we exist but is existence itself, the very power to be.

I like to explain this idea with a science fiction illustration. Imagine a lamp hooked into a power source, spreading warm light across a room. Electricity flows through the cord, and the lamp squeezes light from the raw energy, thanks to Thomas Edison. Now let's step off into the realm of sci-fi for a moment. Suppose there were a power source that not only produced light but generated the lamp as well. Flip a switch, and the power-package causes a lighted lamp to appear. (If you're a *Star Trek* fan, like me, think *holodeck* and you'll have little trouble envisioning this. If not, bear with me a little longer.) Turn off the switch, and the physical lamp, as well as the light, disappears. Energy and matter are the same thing in different form, according to current scientific theory, so the idea of an energy-generated lamp is not entirely beyond possibility. I am not talking about the image of a lamp like a holographic model, but an actual, touchable, solid object, which comes into existence because energy is transmuted into matter. Got it?

Now think about the universe. God is the very power-to-be. Everything exists because God is the energy source that causes everything to exist. "In him we live and move and have our being," said the apostle Paul, paraphrasing Epimenides, the Cretan poet (Acts 17:28). Spirit is the true underlying reality that causes everything to be. The question you should be asking isn't "Does God exist?" but "Why does existence exist?" The answer is because God empowers it to be, provides the principles by which everything operates, and binds the cosmos together in an ongoing learning program, empowered by curiosity, creativity, free will and love. More, God is the principle, energy, learning program—everything. As our Religious Science friends say, *God is all.* Not merely "God is the universe" (pantheism) but "God causes the cosmos to be" (monism). Is that a God to be an atheist about?

You asked about books and practices. I recommend *Remedial Christianity* by Paul A. Laughlin, Ph.D., *anything* by Bishop John Shelby Spong, and the same goes for other members of the Jesus Seminar—Marcus Borg, John Dominic Crossan and the late Robert Funk. For spiritual practices, try *Essential Spirituality* by Roger Walsh, M.D., Ph.D. Dr. Walsh offers lots of practical exercises drawn from most of the major religious traditions of the world. For a readable and modern primer on studying the Bible without fear or confusion read *Wisdom for a Lifetime,* by Alden Studebaker.

One of my favorite stories of the Hebrew Scripture is Jacob wrestling all night with God to obtain a blessing (Genesis 32:24-30). Many people find their path to higher consciousness by meditation and prayer; some of us have to grapple with God. Never apologize for using your mind in spiritual quest; never apologize for the sacred use of the intellect. *Critical thinking* and *creative reflection* mark the path to spiritual insight as clearly any of the tools employed by the feeling nature.

Dear Tom: How can I believe in the integrity of God if I can't believe in my own integrity?
— **K.A., Centerville, Iowa**

Dear K.A.: God's goodness is independent of your highs and lows—but lighten up on yourself, my friend. Everybody has gloomy spells in their moral and spiritual life. Everyone makes mistakes. Once, when I was speaking to a large gathering of spiritually attuned people, I wondered aloud if there were anyone in the audience who would be in jail today if everything he or she had ever done was made known publicly. Although I had meant the question *rhetorically*, almost every hand in the auditorium shot up, and I had to fight the urge to raise mine.

Self-doubt is endemic to the species *Homo sapiens*. People tend to doubt themselves and be their own worst critics. Brahms refused to have his magnificent music published because he felt so overshadowed by Bach and Beethoven. *Can you believe it? Brahms!*

All people fall short of their goals; in fact, that's one of the classic definitions of *sin*. But making mistakes—even really, really bad ones—does not define who you are. You are *imago Dei*, the spiritual image and likeness of God, the divine Spirit within is your true identity, now and forever.

Can you believe in the sun when it isn't shining, the moon when it sets behind the hills? Believe in your essential integrity, even if you don't feel terribly good about yourself at the present time. You have the divine spirit within you, and it will resurface in your consciousness. Meanwhile, act as if it's already back and in full force. This is known as the "fake it until you make it" technique. It works for me.

<blockquote>
Dear Tom: I need and want "light," but I am unable to suspend disbelief or to ignore the hideous, grotesque facts of life in order to embrace, reclaim and trust a loving God. I am quite desperate.

— G.O., Ocean City, New Jersey
</blockquote>

Dear G.O.: If you'll pardon an Information Age analogy, sometimes life feeds us the "wrong programs"—like a computer virus—and we have to "delete the old data and reboot the system." Many of us could point to ugly, objective experiences we've had and say, "You see! Either God doesn't exist or He doesn't care or He's evil!" But that's the "virus program" running. Your task is to identify those "viruses" (some call them *error beliefs*) and "delete" them by using denials/affirmations, then reprogram yourself the same way. You see, our ways of looking at life are entirely *our* choices. You can see the donut, or you can see the hole.

Take the Christmas story as an example: A penniless, middle-aged laborer is forced by a foreign conqueror to travel a hundred miles on foot with his pregnant, teenaged fiancée in the cold of winter, just to pay an oppressive tax. When they arrive, there are no accommodations and they have to live on the street. She is close to delivering, so they take refuge among the animals. After she delivers, they wrap the baby in rags and lay him in a feed trough. Strangers appear in the cold night, demanding to see the child. First, smelly herdsmen arrive, then powerful officials who cannot be denied. The local ruler hears of the baby's birth and sends soldiers to kill all the male children in the town. Even though the mother has just given birth, the family must flee several hundred miles across the barren desert to Egypt, where they live in poverty-stricken exile for years. Now, is that the way you've heard it?

Don't you see that consciousness is an interpretative choice? Try repeating a series of denials followed by affirmations in order to access the new consciousness you're seeking. These thoughts have worked for me: *I deny that sickness, poverty or suffering has any power over me. I am a radiant, spiritual being filled with wisdom, peace and light.* Repeat as often as necessary—hundreds of times a day, if needed—until your system "reboots."

Good Questions

-4-

Prayer Problems and Possibilities

Dear Tom: How is it possible that God can hear and answer millions of prayers at the same time?
— **R.H., Wettingen, Germany**

Dear R.H.: Maybe God listens very quickly? Seriously, the assumption behind your question is that God is like you and me, listening one at a time to each prayer request. But when we realize that God is the one omnipresent Mind, present within all creation and available instantly, a different picture emerges. If God is Supreme Principle rather than a Supreme Being, the principles should work uniformly, everywhere. How does gravity work on earth, if it doesn't work on a distant planet?

Dear Tom: If the Supreme Being is already aware of whatever we might ask, why pray?
— **I.B., Waverly, Ohio**

Dear I.B.: Good question! Why tell God things an omniscient Mind should already know? Is this not a cosmic version of single-player video games? If God is inside each person—if everyone is *imago Dei*, the image and likeness of God—are we essentially talking to ourselves?

Some religious traditions locate prayer somewhere between *begging* and *complaining*, with a little thanksgiving tossed in to sound religious. Prayers of supplication ("O God, if it be Thy will, we beseech Thee to heal, forgive, bless ...") have the unspoken assumption that God's Will is changeable upon a properly worded request. Yet some Christians might legitimately ask, "How could God, who is Absolute Good, want anything but good for me?"

Look to the model of the Psalms. In most instances, prayer is not so much telling *God* what God already knows to be true, but is the psalmist reminding *himself* what God already knows. Psalm 23 ("The Lord is my shepherd, I shall not want") is an affirmation and denial sequence. The psalmist affirms the truth of God's relationship to us and denies all appearances to the contrary. Open the Psalms and you'll find the pattern of affirmation and denial repeated frequently.

The New Testament Lord's Prayer continues and expands on this model: "Give us this day our daily bread. And forgive us our debts, as we also have forgiven our debtors." The use of a possessive pronoun shows the statement is not a merely a request but a claim of ownership—it is "*our* daily bread" for which we pray. The prayer reminds listeners that God's daily supply of human needs is already established. There are places in the world where the flow of this bountiful supply has become constricted, usually by human greed or animosity, but a dry well does not mean water no longer exists. In using the possessive pronoun, Jesus makes a claim that overrules the avarice and belligerence of limited human thinking. The good of the world belongs to its people, and no one should block the channels or divert the course of natural supply.

Metaphysical Christianity holds that prayer benefits the person praying. Think of it as a spiritual alignment that allows the good, which God wants us to have, to flow freely to us. When I taught high school English, the custodian came around and installed a new lock in my classroom door. At first, the shiny key that came with it frequently would not slip into the lock, because the works were slightly misaligned. After the new lock had accepted the new key a few hundred times, it created a grooved pattern, allowing the mechanism to function smoothly.

In the same way, prayer works when we work at it, repeating the process with alacrity and persistently visualizing Truth until the mental mechanisms line up and accept God's key. Sooner or later, this persistency must unlock our true potential and rush splendid results into the padlocked rooms of our lives.

Dear Tom: A hurricane recently threatened the small town where I live. When people in shelters were interviewed, they said that they were praying for their town to be spared. In coastal Mississippi, where the storm later hit, the refugees in the evacuation center were praying for God to spare the Gulf Coast. Both groups were praying for the same outcome. One group was spared; the other suffered hurricane damage. My line of reasoning breaks down here because of two congregations of huddled evacuees, praying to be spared. Only one of them was delivered, but they prayed to the same God with faith.

— J.P., Mandeville, Louisiana

Dear J.P.: I agree. The God they supplicated for redress was flagrantly unfair. That God should have pushed the hurricane out to sea and spared everyone, especially faithful believers who prayed fervently to the Father. But that didn't happen. Why didn't God rush to their aid? Because that God doesn't exist. God isn't "out there" beyond the skies, ready to dip a mighty finger into time and space to set aright the miscarriages of nature and human folly. God is inside the process, not outside. God is the very energy to think, live, love—the power of existence itself. There is no power outside God. Metaphysical Christian pioneer Dr. H. Emilie Cady wrote in *Lessons in Truth* over a century ago:

> God is power. Not simply God has power, but God is power. In other words, all the power there is to do anything is God. God, the source of our existence every moment, is not simply omnipotent (all-powerful); God is omnipotence (all power). God is not alone omniscient (all-knowing); God is omniscience (all knowledge). God is not only omnipresent, but more—omnipresence. God is not a being having qualities, but God is the good itself.[1]

We exist in Divine Mind, in which we live and move and have our being. We are not here to meet a demon-haunted, dangerous world, rescued occasionally by intervention from heaven above. We are here to learn, grow, experience, savor, exult, cherish, create and to use our connection with that Mind to make safe decisions. We are here to share, to be fruitful, and to multiply the good over and over again. Centering on the Divine within, we become still and realize that whatever happens, we are still one with God. Hurricane or sunshine, apparent disaster or celebrated deliverance, God is still absolute Good. James Dillet Freeman's "Prayer for Protection" summarizes the metaphysical Christian understanding of life:

> The light of God surrounds me;
> The love of God enfolds me;
> The power of God protects me;
> The presence of God watches over me.
> Wherever I am, God is![2]

When Jesus Christ faced his hurricane—which did not pass him by—the Man of Nazareth reached beyond himself by finding the Divine within himself. When he prayed, "Thy will be done," it didn't mean he wanted to suffer, but that he recognized God's perfect goodness can be realized in any circumstance. While life's crises may not be manipulated supernaturally, the hurricanes nevertheless lose the power to inflict true, lasting damage on us when we know the divine Truth of God's all-embracing presence and power. Such a mystical vision requires a lot of meditation and prayer before you and I understand it fully, but we'll get it. We have from now to forever, and God is with us every step of the way.

Dear Tom: Your answer to the question about praying to God to be spared from hurricane damage suggests that such prayers are futile because "God isn't 'out there' beyond the skies, ready to dip a mighty finger into time and space to set aright the miscarriages of nature and human folly." Yet Matthew 8:23-27 describes how Jesus, when faced with a severe storm, rebuked the winds and the sea and brought about a great calm. Surely, Jesus calmed the storm by calling on God. Jesus also stated that each one of us has the potential to do whatever he did. Please clarify.
— **W.H., Fairport, New York**

Dear W.H.: You have raised a deeply *metaphysical* issue, and I am using the word here not in the popular sense but with a theological-philosophic connotation: metaphysics as the study of the underlying structure of reality. I don't know whether my answer will satisfy you completely, but let's give it a shot.

The question you've asked is essentially this: How is the activity of God realized in the physical world? There are some fundamental assumptions which must be adequately examined to grapple with the problem. Is existence natural, or supernatural? There seem to be three possible answers. First, naturalistic materialism. One could reject the existence of anything spiritual, period. Nothing outside of space-time exists, and no unseen spiritual forces are at work in the world. There may be powerful unseen forces which humans can tap into, but these are nonsentient and subject to the same scientific principles which govern the rest of the cosmos.

A second possibility is a dualism of spirit and matter, with God ruling both. In this metaphysical system, the Divine has All-Power and can do anything. God and the cosmos are separate and unequal, and God chooses what He (usually male) wants by some inscrutable networking within the Godhead. In most metaphysical dualisms, God is spared the charge of whimsy by being an All-Good, All-Loving Supreme Being whose decrees are therefore beyond criticism.

The third possibility is a bit more difficult to describe because it requires a different way of thinking about Ultimate Reality. *Metaphysical Christianity,* as it is often called, sees the cosmos as functioning by certain spiritual principles programmed into the fabric of reality. These principles have been called "law" in previous generations, but science today is less convinced that the cosmos operates mechanically. Since Einstein, the line between matter and energy has become fuzzy—are humans physical beings or localized complexes of energy? Is consciousness based in energy or matter, or is there even a difference?

What this suggests is that the cosmos is hooked together in a way both miraculous and natural. Can a person pray and change the outcome through natural intervention? Maybe that's the wrong question. Maybe a better way of looking at the interaction of people and events is to see human consciousness linked to Divine Mind, and inasmuch as we are capable of allowing the Divine to out-picture through us, that is the degree to which we express what looks like power, mastery and dominion in mind, body and affairs in this level of existence. However—and this is the key point for metaphysical Christianity—it wasn't by contacting some deity in the clouds that Jesus was able to still the storm. He exercised power by realizing his oneness with the storm, with the world and with the Divine Mind behind the process. He was not manipulating God; he was realizing his Oneness with God, and through that realization Jesus was able to ride the storm to its natural culmination.

Can you and I do this? Not yet. Very few people have reached that degree of certainty, which is probably a good thing for the orderliness of this world. However, I am absolutely certain that you and I will eventually realize our oneness with God to the degree reached by Jesus, and then go beyond even that level to—who knows what? I don't know about you, but the journey ahead excites and comforts me. Peace, be still. We'll all get there.

Dear Tom: How do you know when God is talking to you rather than when you're having random thoughts?
— J.X., Wichita, Kansas

Dear J.X.: Listen carefully. If your "guidance" is nutty, hostile, plaintive, shrill, mean-spirited, discouraging or full of anxiety—it's not God. Nothing but good comes from God. So if what you are hearing in your mind is *good*, you're probably safe in assuming God is the Source.

Dear Tom: We are told to say in the Lord's Prayer, "Our Father who art in heaven ..." Then we are told "the kingdom of God is within—in which case we would be praying to ourselves. I am confused.
— **A.E., Oakland, California**

Dear A.E.: I have this conversation regularly with folks who are confused about how to "locate" God. Is there a "Father-Mother God" in heaven, or is the Divine within us? Some mystics have said we find God only within ourselves, yet other spiritual teachers say God is omnipresent and therefore can also be discovered beyond the self in the cosmos. In the best traditions of systematic theology, my response is "yes and no" to both positions. I certainly believe God is "out there" in the universe, available at every location. In *Lessons in Truth*, H. Emilie Cady says that God is not only all-present; in fact, God is Omnipresence Itself. However—and here is where it gets a little tricky—everything experienced in the "outer" is really being experienced in the "inner" consciousness.

The ink on this printed page, by which you are seeing my words, does not hop off the paper in your hands and invade your eyes, nerves and brain. Your sensory system reaches out and perceives the ink marks; you then interpret this "report" inside the cockpit of your consciousness.

So, yes; God is everywhere—inside, outside. But even when you feel the Divine Presence in an outside event like a majestic mountain vista or a glorious sunset over the sea, you are experiencing the Divine from within you.

About "praying to ourselves" ... How about simply reminding oneself of what is true by the use of affirmative prayer? "The Lord is my shepherd; I shall not want ..."

-5-

Process Theology

Dear Tom: Next to the nature of God, nothing has intrigued me more than the subject of predestination. Yet it has also weakened my faith that we are the captains of our fate. For example, I've had a precognitive dream. Does this mean life is like watching a movie?

— **J.F., California (no city provided)**

Dear J.F.: The real problem lodges in your other favorite topic—the nature of God. Can you believe the universe is a computer program that God left running while taking a nap? That's where you end up with the doctrine of predestination. The logic goes like this: God knows everything. Therefore, 20 billion years ago, sitting in the dark, God knew exactly what I was going to write on this page, knew you would pick up the book, and knew what you'd think when you read my words. So freedom is an illusion. Now, the terrifying danger in this doctrine is that any deed becomes God's doing: slavery, the Holocaust, poverty, child abuse, terminal diseases—need I continue? Predestination descends quickly into fatalism, which makes it easy to shun one's responsibility in life, which is the polar opposite of the message of Jesus Christ.

Let me share a lovely, heretical idea I've been playing with for several years. Maybe God knows everything—all the possible combinations of all your possible choices—*except* the choice you actually make. Maybe God gave the cosmos the gift of choice in that primordial act of creation 15 to 20 billion years ago.

Besides, it really doesn't matter. Whether the underlying metaphysical reality has produced people who have total freedom or actors playing their part in a cosmic drama—the point is that I *experience* life as freedom, and that's how I must live. Even in a movie, actors can't stop the projector and call for a rewrite.

Dear Tom: If God is perfect and changeless, does God become stagnant? Or does God grow and change?
— **M.D., Jonesboro, Georgia**

Dear M.D.: Your question breaks new ground, and the answer will require some heavy-duty thinking. In previous generations, it was blasphemous to suggest that God can change. How could the all-mighty, all-potent, all-knowing deity transform into something else? The thought is a little scary. Yet there are responsible Christian theologians today who contend that God does change, even grows. The school of thought which holds this view is called *process theology*; its chief advocates are the intellectual heirs to the work of Alfred North Whitehead (1861–1947). Whitehead was a rather ponderous yet profound thinker who began as a philosopher of mathematics then moved on to religion.

Whitehead believed that God is not a static entity but an evolving *process*. In fact, Whitehead argued that all consciousness is a process. You were once an infant, then a child, adolescent and young adult. Which of these stages is you? Obviously, all of them, as well as all the stages of life you have yet to experience. You change and grow, yet every stage of your existence is an authentic out-picturing of your real self. Whitehead held that God is so integrated into the fabric of reality that God experiences this progression of thoughts, feelings and day-by-day activities in all sentient beings.

But how does God change? Process theologians would say that by participating in the events of your life and the existence of all sentient beings, God gains more experiences. By receiving and giving love, God absorbs those exchanges and "realizes" the increased love. T. A. Kantonen describes the God of process theology:

> Far from being enthroned in remote, solitary splendor, he [God] is a responsive and responsible give-and-take relation to the world. He receives, treasures, and remembers everything that happens and uses it to further his purpose of cosmic advance from the potential to the actual. In Whitehead's own words, he is "the fellow-sufferer who understands," and in him our perishing experiences "live forevermore."[1]

The idea that God is a process is highly controversial in Christian theology. At first glance, it also seems out of step with metaphysical Christianity, which has always held that God is "Absolute Good." But the word *absolute* doesn't have to mean "changeless." It can mean "total" or "endless" as well. I'm not sure I agree with everything process theologians say, but I'd like to think that my interactions with the Divine can in some way add to the total good of the cosmos. For more on divine transformation, read on.

Dear Tom: Good parents give a lot of consideration to teaching their children and, perhaps more importantly, learning from them. Since God is omniscient, is it ludicrous to think that God might learn from His children?
— **J.R., San Lorenzo, California**

Dear J.R.: Not at all! If God has truly given us free will, we must have the power to surprise God with our choices. One school of Christian thought, process theology, says that God is the whole process in which we exist and that God grows as we make choices and experience life. Isn't it limiting God to say He/She/It cannot learn, cannot be surprised, and cannot grow?

Dear Tom: According to Old Testament scripture, God changed His mind. I have even heard members of the clergy say that His mind can be changed through prayer. I believe that God is immutable

Spirit with which we align our spirits, not vice versa. I would appreciate your response to bolster (I hope) my side of the argument.
— **E.T., Glenford, Ohio**

Dear E.T.: I hate to disappoint you, but there's a possible "yes and no" answer to your question. Read on.

Dear Tom: Are you a process theology person? Can you tell me what to read to help me make sense of that?
— **L.H., Clearwater, Florida**

Dear L.H.: Yes, I'm a process theologian—although not in an absolute sense. Process theology says God is not constrained by time and space; God is the whole process of life, evolution, time and space. Here's a specific example: You have pictures of yourself as an infant, toddler, grade schooler, teen, young adult and so on, correct? If your life pattern continues normally, you'll have photos of yourself as an octogenarian someday. Lay them out chronologically—which one would you say is you? The answer is, of course, *all of them*. You are not a slice in time; you are a *process*.

Process theology says, *so is God*. A metaphysical Christian way to put it would be to see Divine Mind as the very process by which all the other processes are empowered to express and become. Consequently, as the process unfolds, God *grows*. As the cosmos expresses itself in creative diversity,

God *experiences* new events. God *changes* by experiencing that which creative freedom of the cosmos co-creates with its empowering share of the divine energy. Yet there may be another level, above the God-concept of process theology. Even the process must operate by certain principles. One could argue, in a Platonic sense, that the *principles* which guide the divine creative process are the true God-behind-God. Some metaphysical thinkers have insisted that God is not a being and can be better understood as Divine Principle.

For further reference, take a look at the work of husband-and-wife team C. Alan Anderson and Deborah G. Whitehouse.

Dear Tom: I am interested in the term *process theology,* for I had never heard of it before. I found your brief explanation [above] quite interesting. However, I have another point of view. To me, the main problem with most theological concepts, including, apparently, process theology, is that they personify the Creator-Sustainer concept. When man does that, he limits the Creator concept by placing it within a time, space and form continuum. I believe that when the Creator-Sustainer concept is given the limits of time, space and form, it ceases to be absolute. I would offer a concept of the Creator-Sustainer that is limitless and timeless, without any form of descriptive expression: Infinite Principle and Presence—Infinite Principle as Divine Mind, Infinite Presence as the Eternal Now. To me, God neither grows nor becomes stagnant, because there is nothing to change if God is absolute perfection—which also rules out stagnation.

— **R.L., Bisbee, Arizona**

Dear R.L.: You're correct when you say God is beyond any image or concept we humans can design. Twentieth-century theologian Paul Tillich said that everything we say about God is symbolic. Tillich insists we must continue to think of God as personal, even though we know that God utterly transcends the limitations of personality, finitude and being. Why? Because human beings are *persons*, therefore relate to the cosmos *personally*. Some metaphysical writers see God as impersonal. I agree, but only if the impersonal nature of God is greater than personal, not less. I like to think of God as *transpersonal*. As I've said in other writings, the question is not "Shall we worship the true God or an idol?" The question is "Which idol shall we worship?" Which word-picture of the utterly inexplicable shall we paint?

Process theology—which holds that God is an unfolding process—provides some answers to questions about the nature of reality, but it is not identical with Ultimate Truth. As you imply in your eloquent and thought-provoking letter, no human system of thought can totally apprehend, comprehend and reprehend the Divine.

-6-

The Soul

Dear Tom: My question is—What actually is the difference between the soul and the spirit of a person? The only reference to it I have ever found is in H. Emilie Cady's *Lessons in Truth* where she writes: "In our out-springing from God into the material world, Spirit is inner—one with God; soul is the clothing, as it were, of the Spirit; body is the external clothing of the soul."[1]

This is lovely, but does not really answer my question. I would greatly appreciate your thoughts on this.

— **P.H., Winston-Salem, North Carolina**

Dear P.H.: Your answer is contained in that quote from Dr. Cady. She wrote in word-symbols, which were understood by her audience at the beginning of the 20th century but sound alien to us today. Symbolic language varies among religious groups, so *Spirit* means one thing to Protestant Pentecostals and quite another to Greek Orthodox Christians.

As I see it, Unity thinkers reserve the word *Spirit* to mean the eternal, unchanging divine Presence within each person.

That part of God which you are, have been, and always will be—that shard of Divinity which is the real you—that is your Spirit. It is your direct link to Divine Mind.

Soul is a trickier term because it's used interchangeably with *Spirit* in many theologies. However, metaphysical Christianity tends to see *soul* as practically synonymous with the human mind; your soul reflects the current state of your progress on the journey toward realizing your oneness with God.

Some metaphysicians say *body* is the outpouring of the soul and reflects our thoughts about ourselves, but I tend to agree with those who hold this formula: *Body* is a product of the natural world; *soul* has a foot in both kingdoms—spiritual and physical; *Spirit* is wholly divine. If these ideas don't work for you, try meditating on the terms to learn directly from the Source—the Divine Mind within you. And remember, symbolic theology usually sounds good only to the person who clangs the symbols.

Dear Tom: My mother made her transition recently, at the age of 90, after seven years of dementia. For the last three to four years of her life, she knew none of her family, nor even who she herself was. What I have puzzled over for, lo, these many years, is where has she been? I mean, her mind has obviously not been with her, but the essence of her— where has it been? I have pondered this, prayed, had nightmares about it, tossed and turned, and no answers have come.

— J.I., Sunset Valley, Texas

Dear J.I.: That's another great question, not asked previously. Where did your mom go when suffering from dementia? It's only a problem because you're thinking dualistically—God is *there*; I am *here*. God is not me. Try recalibrating your thinking to see God as the One Presence and One Power. Think of the human mind as a receiver and Divine Mind as the sender (This isn't a perfect analogy, but let's play with it.) If a radio is damaged, what happens to the signal it receives? If a car radio is destroyed in a wreck, is the transmitting station knocked off the air? Let's look at other analogies. If the ground is saturated with rain, does it stop the clouds from showering? If you fall into a cave, does your mishap blacken the sun?

You can find your own examples now. The point is, if the brain is the physical receiver, which allows your body to express a limited out-picturing of the Infinite Mind, then brain damage will affect the receiver but not the Sender. You will still be who you are, because you are a bit of Divinity. However, you won't be able to express as much of your true nature—Divinity—because the receiver has been damaged. Think of plants and animals. Are they not examples of the same life-force that animates humans? Your mother didn't go anywhere; she was simply less able to express her Oneness with God than she previously could.

Dear Tom: I've always wondered if my cat (and I guess all animals in general) has a soul like people do? I am very close to my cat, and it seems to me that my cat does have a soul, but I wonder if there is any literature that supports my belief.
— **L.R., Colorado (no city provided)**

Dear L.R.: Absolutely! My favorite author, Yorkshire veterinarian Dr. James Herriot, assured his cat-loving clients that animals do indeed have souls. Also, in her book *Embraced by the Light*, Betty J. Eadie says that during her near-death experience her out-of-body soul whirled along a tunnel where she became aware of other people and animals traveling with her at a distance. And check this out, from the book of Ecclesiastes:

> For the fate of humans and the fate of animals is the same; as one dies, so dies the other. They all have the same breath, and humans have no advantage over the animals; for all is vanity. ... Who knows whether the human spirit goes upward and the spirit of animals goes downward to the earth? (Ecclesiastes 3:19, 21)

I can't imagine God allowing you to live in eternity without your cat. But please, when we get there, come to visit me alone. I like cats, but they make me sneeze!

-7-

Evil Is a Four-Letter Word

Dear Tom: I try to be good, but sometimes I just do bad things. Why do I keep doing wrong? I feel bad but can't seem to stop!
— **Internet Question (no name given)**

Dear Friend: If you could see the heads nodding across the world as people read your plaintive letter, you'd know you are not alone. Sometimes people feel locked into cycles of self-destructive behavior and despair of finding our way out of the maze. No less than the apostle Paul himself felt something close to the anguish you describe: "I do not understand my own actions. For I do not do what I want, but I do the very thing I hate" (Romans 7:15).

I believe that one of the reasons God created the cosmos was to express conscious, creative creatures, like you and me, who would learn to do what is right. People learn by trial and error. Sometimes, lots of error. Let me assure you: God holds no grudges, wields no sword of retribution, and punishes no one. What you're doing to yourself is punishment enough. Now let's see if we can get you beyond it.

First, go find a competent spiritual counselor—minister, priest or rabbi. Someone trained in pastoral counseling will be able to hear your pain and suggest concrete steps you can take to break the cycle. Next, pray without ceasing. Tell God what you feel—all of it. Don't hold back. Dump the whole load into God's hands. When we feel as if we are being crucified, remember what the symbolism of the Crucifixion means: even in the most desperate circumstances, God has everything under control, despite all appearances to the contrary.

Finally, find something you can do that makes you feel good about yourself. Sing in the choir. Hand out sandwiches and soup at the local shelter. Volunteer at the veterans' hospital or middle school library or community center. Never quit believing that you are the precious child of God. See yourself as God sees you, filled with wisdom, peace and light—a work in progress.

Dear Tom: I've always wondered about the "unforgivable sin" which Jesus says will never be pardoned. It's mentioned three of the four Gospels. What is it, and how can I tell if I'm guilty of this eternal sin?
— G.W., Colorado (no city provided)

Dear G.W.: You are not the first person to fret over this peculiar passage of Scripture. Nearly every minister has had a parishioner wander into the pastor's study after Sunday coffee hour to ask some variation on this question: "Have I committed a sin which cannot be forgiven?"

Evil Is a Four-Letter Word

It's a straightforward question that demands an honest answer: "No! That's not what the Bible teaches." The word *blasphemy* comes from two Greek words (*blaptein*, "to injure," and *pheme*, "reputation"). According to the *New Advent Catholic Encyclopedia*, the word *blasphemy* signifies "gross irreverence towards any person or thing worthy of exalted esteem." Although it usually refers to deprecation of the divine, the word has a wider sense; Roger Bacon spoke of "blasphemy against learning."[1]

In the synoptic Gospels, Jesus identifies blasphemy against "the Holy Spirit" as an "unforgivable sin":

> Truly I tell you, people will be forgiven for their sins and whatever blasphemies they utter; but whoever blasphemes against the Holy Spirit can never have forgiveness, but is guilty of an eternal sin"—for they had said, "He has an unclean spirit" (Mark 3:28-30).

A basic premise of biblical studies today is that the Gospels are neither the transcribed notes of eyewitnesses nor consolidated histories in the modern sense. The Bible is an *anthology*, a library of recorded memories, and the individual "books" were shaped by the communities of faith which produced them. Rather than news reports, the Gospels are more like teaching materials, like Sunday school booklets produced by a denominational publisher. There is history in the story, but the narrative is wrapped in a point of view which has shaped all the characters and events. Although there was only one Jesus of Nazareth, Matthew's Jesus is not Luke's Jesus, and neither is anything like John's.

The question therefore becomes what does *blasphemy against the Holy Spirit* mean to the author of the text? If you look at the context of all three Gospels where this story is related, Jesus is responding to a charge that his power comes from "an unclean spirit" or some other demonic force. Since the authors of the Gospels are unanimous that Jesus was a spiritual being, the thought that he could be functioning from some center of evil was utterly repugnant to all the Christian communities. Mark, the oldest Gospel, repudiates this denigration of Jesus' inner spirit in the strongest terms possible— *no way, not now, not ever!*

Some biblical scholars suspect there is a layer of universalism in the teachings of the historical Jesus which can be glimpsed beneath this extreme statement. There is no way to know, since the Gospel stories were handed down through many editors and shaped by the social, political and theological forces of the Judeo-Hellenistic world. However, the idea that anyone could be lost without hope of redemption is so out of synch with other statements by Jesus that serious questions can be raised about the historicity of these "unforgivable sin" passages.

For a metaphysical interpretation of the passage, which requires creative interaction with the words of the text, Charles Fillmore wrote that blasphemy means "impious or irreverent thoughts toward God, such as sickness, poverty, death."[2] As long as we continue denying the ultimate power of Spirit in all things, we cannot receive the blessings (that is, forgiveness) that are rightfully ours as children of a loving God.

Now for the Gospel (which means "good news"): As soon as we accept God's presence and power as supreme in our lives, the floodgates are rolled open and divine blessings shower upon us like a cloudburst in the desert. Actually, God doesn't turn goodness off and on; it's always raining down on us. Only our continued denial of health, prosperity and life eternal can keep us from our good. When we quit rejecting our acceptance, we cease "sinning" against the Spirit and therefore stop committing the "unforgivable sin" and are reconciled to God's eternal forgiveness.

Dear Tom: I have heard spiritual teachers say that God doesn't love anyone; God is love. Your thoughts?
— K.D., Columbus, Ohio

Dear K.D.: If you mean, "Is there a Supreme Being out there beyond time and space, a God separate from His creation which He nevertheless loves?"—then I have to agree with the "God doesn't love" crowd. Here's something I wrote for *Contact* magazine, which I believe speaks to the heart of your question:

> What if *God* is just another way of saying *Existence Itself*? What if God is not a Supreme Being but a Supreme Process? What if reality is not governed by some distant Creator who dwells unchangeably in Heaven, unable to do anything but admire His static perfection? What

if the cosmos is God in action, an expression of divine energy, a flurry of colors flying from the brush of the Creative Artist, and we are those colors, and we are that Artist? What if everything is in God, and God is in everything, in all Its myriad forms and expressions and possibilities?[3]

Now there are those who say we should not pray to or think about a God "out there" because it diminishes our understanding of the God-within, but this to me sounds like another variation of the "unpardonable sin" argument (see above), in that any devotion or recognition of God-in-the-World is a form of idolatry, a rejection of the true nature of the Divine. Sorry, but for me that's pushing it too far. Even though I believe God is the energy by which everything lives, moves and has its being, I still need to stand under a starry sky and allow myself the luxury of feeling *loved* by God, the Good, Omnipotent.

Dear Tom: While going through some papers a while back, I came upon a question I had written in 1978: "If Jesus died for our sins, then why, if death is the wages of sin, do we die, if he died for our sins?" After reading this column for several years, I think I know your answer.
— R.B., Inman, South Carolina

Dear R.B.: Then you're way ahead of me, friend, because I'm not sure how to answer this question yet! You are actually paraphrasing two biblical quotations: "God proved his love for us in that while we still were sinners Christ died for us" (Romans 5:8). "For the wages of sin is death, but the free gift of God is eternal life in Christ Jesus our Lord" (Romans 6:23).

I guess I could pick at the syntax, play with the words "die for our sins" and substitute a little metaphysical tap dance to soothe the impact of Paul's affirmation. But instead, let's take Paul seriously enough to investigate what he probably was saying to his target audience. To make sense of these passages, we're going to have to dig into the historical background of the Bible.

It is clear from New Testament sources and other early documents that many first-century Christians saw the death of Jesus on the cross as an act comparable to sacrificing an animal to appease Zeus, Apollo or some other god.

We shouldn't be too hard on them. Disease, famine, war and mundane tragedies were far more prevalent than today. People thought the gods were intimately involved with and easily offended by human actions and, consequently, needed to be placated regularly. And, they reasoned, since every blessing and misfortune in life originates in supernatural activity—for example, the gods send the rain or withhold it— that means the seemingly endless plagues of daily life must come from divine displeasure at human disobedience; in other words, sin. Although various cultures defined the consequences of sin differently, most ancient religions, including the Hebrew faith, solved the problem of divine displeasure by ritually killing animals. Blood sacrifice, they believed, was the only way to avoid calamity in this life and destruction of the soul, eternal punishment, or a lethargic nonexistence

(Greek, *Hades*) in the life to come. So our ancestors spilled the blood of animals to avoid shedding their own blood through misfortunes brought about by divine wrath. They also shared a large portion of the meat with the priests who killed the beasts. In fact, the back doors of pagan temples often functioned as butcher shops and earned a good income for the religious institution.

When the people of the Christian community were struggling to understand the meaning of the death of Jesus, they looked out the window at the temples dotting the Greco-Roman hillsides. Hellenistic Christians, who had grown up as pagans, knew that in many of those temples animals were ritually slain every day as a way of restoring harmony between the individual offender (sinner) and the annoyed deity. Jewish Christians, who had grown up within the Hebrew faith, also knew that animal sacrifices were commanded by the God of Israel as a sin offering from the people. The temple at Jerusalem was awash in the blood of rams, bulls, doves and lambs. It was a ghastly spectacle.

But now comes Jesus, and—against his expressed wishes—he is hailed by followers as Messiah, the Anointed One (in Greek, *Christos*). And then he is *killed*? What meaning can we ascribe to the death of God's chosen one? Imagine the cognitive dissonance his followers must have felt. To put the problem the way they may have framed it:

- Jesus was sent by God, therefore God was with him.
- God was with him, therefore God's righteousness would insure Jesus' mission against failure.
- Jesus got himself crucified, dead and buried. That must have been part of God's plan.

- Since it was God's will, the death of Jesus could *not* have been a failure, but must be a hidden good.

- What therefore did Jesus accomplish by freely accepting death upon the cross?

"Of course!" the early Church said. *"He is the lamb of God, Whose death takes away the sin of the whole world."* This interpretation offered a number of advantages. First, it transformed utter failure into crowing glory. Second, the image of a sacrificial offering to the divine was a universal motif in religions of the ancient world. Jews and pagans alike practiced animal sacrifice to restore the balance between heaven and earth. The death of Jesus as the universal sacrifice to bridge the gap once and for all would be understood by everyone, everywhere. It was a brilliant move.

Paul said that although the wages of human misbehavior are paid in death and nonexistence (Paul doesn't subscribe to eternal punishment), faith in the Christ frees the individual believer for eternal life through his sacrifice. Paul's solution was just one possible interpretation of the "work" of Jesus Christ. Other interpretations, which promised eternal hell for nonbelievers, were heavily influenced by Jewish Apocalypticism, Gnostic dualism and pagan ideas of the afterlife that were prevalent in the culture at the time.

But if we look at the life events and actual teachings of Jesus, we find very little to support any of these theories. Jesus did not call people to worship him; he called people to follow him on the path to God, in other words, higher consciousness. If there was any meaning to his life and work, it was as an example of what it means to trust God despite all appearances to the contrary.

Now, about the "why do we die" part—because it is the doorway to the next phase of life. To move on, you have to pack your bags and clear out of the place where you're living. Death is not punishment for sin; it's the gateway to the next level. See you on the other side—if not sooner!

Dear Tom: Are people born as original sinners?
— L.C.D., Detroit, Michigan

Dear L.C.D.: Some traditions say we are, but metaphysical Christianity doesn't see people as having a sinful nature; essential human character is usually described in terms of freedom. In classical terms, *sin* means "missing the mark; that is, falling short of divine perfection."[4] It is important to note that when people make a "mistake" in their learning process, they can learn from the error too. Sometimes this is hard to accept, because people can make some violent, hateful, disruptive choices. One could argue those decisions come from an inherently evil streak within humans, or see it as making a maladaptive choice.

Sin is also sometimes defined as *any attempt to negate a divine idea* (popularized by the late, great metaphysician Ed Rabel). For example, *theft* is an attempt to negate the divine idea of *abundance*; *murder* is the attempt to negate the divine idea of *life*; *racism, sexism* and *homophobia* are attempts to negate the divine idea of *the Christ within* every person. I seldom speak of *good versus evil* but, rather, see the world in terms of growth and nongrowth. Although one cannot deny that evil deeds are done by people, free will does not mean that evil has any existential reality. H. Emilie Cady wrote a cogent summary:

> *There is no evil.* There is but one power in the universe, and that is God—Good. God is good, and God is omnipresent. Apparent evils are not entities or things of themselves. They are simply an apparent absence of the good, just as darkness is an absence of light. But God, or good, is omnipresent, so the apparent absence of good (evil) is unreal. It is only an appearance of evil, just as the moving sun was an appearance.[5]

Evil is not a force but, as Cady says in the above passage, an "apparent absence of the good, just as darkness is an absence of light." This viewpoint is fairly typical of metaphysical Christianity today. I have also heard evil defined as a sense of separation from God, created in mind. Since God as Absolute Good is omnipresent, what actually exists is the mind's misperception of separation from God.

To me, *evil* is a four-letter word, a powerful concept which taken out of context can cause great conflict. Of course, there are *evil* deeds. Who could look at the pictures of Holocaust survivors and say everything is *good-good-good*? But the fact that people make mistakes—even horrific, monstrous mistakes—does not change human basic nature as children of God. People are not hell-bound sinners in need of a savior, but students in need of a Master. Fortunately, the great religions of the world have provided a cadre of master teachers to guide humanity on its upward climb from the primeval slime to the space-faring, love-centered culture which I believe we are intended to be. The list of guides along the journey include prophets and teachers like Buddha, Zoroaster, Mohammed and more recently, Baha'u'llah. In the Western tradition, Judaism looks to Moses, Abraham and the Prophets, plus its great teachers and scholars of the Torah, and the Christian faith directs people to an encounter with another master teacher in Jesus of Nazareth, who demonstrated by his life, teachings and resurrection experience what it means to be one with God. All these teachers have called people to follow the upward path. Any evil we may encounter along the way is a detour, not a force, power or destination.

-8-

Hell, No ...

Dear Tom: What do you believe about hell or sinning?
— **M.K., Elk Grove, California**

Dear M.K.: We choose both; neither is required, or lasts forever, or has any power over us, or exists in reality. We can choose to put ourselves in hell mentally. It's not sin that gets us there, it's sin that keeps us from departing. We can choose to board the Mind-shuttle to heaven. When people realize that God loves them unconditionally, all hell breaks loose.

Dear Tom: I would like to know your thoughts on hell. My thinking is that a God who is all good couldn't create hell.
— **R.O.D., Yuma, Arizona**

Dear R.O.D.: Right. Besides, the monthly energy bill would be hellacious.

Dear Tom: I recently had a heated discussion with my mother about hell. She believes in the literal interpretation of hell as a burning pit where everyone who has not accepted Jesus as Savior goes to suffer for eternity. I was raised in a conservative church but became a student of Unity at age 18. I'm now 54, and still occasionally have to remind myself how ludicrous this belief in hell really is. Anyway, I remember reading something several years ago that gave the Aramaic interpretation of the word *hell* as a place to dispose of trash or burning refuse. I tried to explain to my mother that I believed this meant a place for us to dispose of our negative thoughts or bad habits rather than literally letting people burn alive for eternity. Could you help me out on this Aramaic interpretation, give me your views on the subject of hell as a place, and also tell me where this term *saved* came from? The concept that only those who believe in Jesus as God's Son will be accepted into His kingdom makes God sound so petty and small. The God I have in my heart wouldn't do that!

— **P.J., Waynesville, Missouri**

Dear P.J.: Yeesh! There are volumes of theology written on several of the subquestions you've asked. At the risk of massive oversimplification, which I have never neglected to commit whenever possible, here goes ...

Not Aramaic. Despite what the lonely advocates of George Lamsa believe, the vast bulk of New Testament scholarship says the canonical Christian Scriptures were not written in Aramaic but in the international language of the day Koine Greek. The word usually translated as *hell* in English Bibles is *Gehenna*, which is a Greek version of the Hebrew word *gehinnom*, literally, *the valley of Hinnom*. This was a ravine outside the ancient city walls where pre-Hebrew inhabitants supposedly offered human sacrifices, an act that rendered the ground ritually unclean for Jewish purposes. Consequently, Gehenna became the city dump of Jerusalem, as you mentioned, where trash and refuse was burned. It was a smoldering wasteland, reeking of decay and sulfuric fumes. When New Testament writers wanted to explain what it was like to cut yourself off from the goodness of God, they could not have picked a better image.

To the term *savior* we also have better recourse. The word in the Greek, *soter*, which is usually rendered *savior* in English New Testaments, can also be translated *healer*. This means that whenever the Bible says Jesus saved us or Jesus is our savior, the acceptable alternative translation also applies: Jesus *healed* us; Jesus is our *healer*. Hence, the title of Charles Fillmore's book *Jesus Christ Heals* is an alternative translation of ... You got it!

About hell itself: Taken literally, it's a monstrous absurdity. Imagine a place where sentient beings are tortured for all eternity because they didn't make the right choices for 70-plus years on earth. What parent would torture his children, anyway? Is punishment not supposed to have a corrective, rehabilitative element to it? Beyond all this, a literal, burning hell represents an affront to the ecology and economy of God's creation. The sulfur indicates a pollution source, which must continue into eternity, and the heating bill alone would make the whole business cost-prohibitive.

But you'll probably do better not trying to convince your mom on this point. Some folks are uncomfortable without a doctrine of eternal punishment, but only God knows why ...

Dear Seekers of Truth: I have studied your magazine for the past three issues, and I remain puzzled. Thomas Shepherd was asked if it is necessary to accept Jesus Christ to avoid being destroyed in hell. Mr. Shepherd answered that hell is a "state of mind." Mr. Shepherd added that God has individual plans for each person to achieve spiritual growth. You claim to teach mankind the truth taught by Jesus Christ. But if you believe it is not necessary to accept Jesus Christ in order to obtain salvation, then you don't believe in the Bible.
— E.T., Lanham, Maryland

Dear E.T.: You have accurately reproduced the gist of my comments, but I take issue with the claim that a Christian interpretation which embraces universalism means disbelief in the Bible. First, all honest biblical interpretation begins with the frank admission that human beings have changed their attitudes in the centuries since the Bible was written. What rational person today believes in slavery, the flat earth theory, or holy slaughter in God's name—all supported in Scripture? (See Exodus 21:2; 1 Corinthians 7:21-24; Ephesians 6:5-8; Deuteronomy 28:64, 30:4; Nehemiah 1:9; Job 28:24; Joshua 8:24-29.)

More important, the Bible was never intended to be an absolute, unbending law code. It is an anthology of ancient writings, preserving memories of the Hebrew and Christian communities in story, legend, myth, wisdom literature, poetry, prayers, letters and sacred histories that evolved as living documents, subject to re-evaluation and reinterpretation.

In one example of a New Testament author's attitude toward Scripture, Luke, the author of Luke and Acts, shows an encounter between the apostle Philip and an Ethiopian eunuch. The gentile official was reading from a scroll of the prophet Isaiah while riding in a carriage. Philip ran over and asked him, "Do you understand what you are reading?" The Ethiopian replied, "How can I, unless someone guides me?" (Acts 8:30-31). It was a request for reinterpretation, for textual analysis, which the Christian community at the time was applying to the Jewish Scriptures to discover passages that Christians believed pointed to Jesus as the messiah of the Jews and lord of the gentiles. Of course, rabbis to this day disagree. But the process of re-evaluation and reinterpretation is absolutely essential to a living faith. On this point, Christian and Jew have always agreed, in theory, if not in practice.

Jesus Christ spoke the language of his thought-world, but we must not hold those high spiritual insights hostage to an ancient, mythological view of the cosmos. As both a Christian theologian and teacher of theological ethics, I am convinced there is no literal hell, but there are plenty of people whose self-defeating choices in life (that is, abusive behavior towards self or others) have landed them in a hell-on-earth. It is from this pedestrian perdition that faith in Jesus Christ can deliver us. We can otherwise trust eternity to God's hands, regardless of which religious faith we may practice.

Dear Tom: Thanks to *Unity Magazine* for helpful words and instruction. My Anglican faith is enhanced by its flavor. Some fundamentalist Christians tell me that if I don't accept Jesus Christ as my personal Lord and Savior, I will most certainly be destroyed in hell. I don't believe in hell! What will I say to them? They are good people too.
— **J.B., Hampton, Nova Scotia, Canada**

Dear J.B.: Greetings to our friends in Nova Scotia. You might take comfort in the fact that, outside the fundamentalist circles, there are virtually no modern theologians who talk about hell as a place of eternal punishment. Since you're an Anglican, let me invoke my favorite English churchman, Professor John Macquarrie. Writing in the 1960s, Macquarrie disparaged "the barbarous doctrine of an eternal hell" and spoke in favor of "universalism," in which all sentient beings would eventually be united with God. I quote this highly distinguished orthodox theologian at length:

> Needless to say, we utterly reject the idea of a hell where God everlastingly punishes the wicked, without hope of deliverance. Even earthly penologists are more enlightened nowadays. Rather we must believe that God will never cease from his quest for universal reconciliation, and we can firmly hope for his victory in this quest, through recognizing that this victory can only come when at last there is the free cooperation of every responsible creature.[1]

In other words, hell isn't a place; it's a state of mind. If we persist in "sin," doing things we know to be against God's intention for us, we take ourselves further and further off the path to oneness with God. Of course, God accompanies us as we wander among the briars and the weeds, but that's not where we're supposed to be. I believe God has given each of us an individualized instruction program to achieve maximum spiritual growth. The plan won't be the same for you and me. Some people need more structure, others need more freedom; some people thrive when challenged by hardship, others require stability and long periods of quiet reflection.

Your fundamentalist friends don't need to be convinced that there is no hell. They need to be blessed, released and sent forward to find their highest good. Sooner or later, if they need that bit of knowledge for their spiritual growth, they'll discover it by themselves.

Dear Tom: I feel compelled to write after reading your comments to J.B. in your column concerning hell. That writer professed disbelief in an eternal hell, and to my amazement—you agreed! What kind of a cult are you people?
— **B.M., Marysville, Ohio**

Dear B.M.: Oh, come on now. Just because you disagree with a theological viewpoint doesn't make the other side evil. The early Christian church was accused of wild, cultic practices by Roman authorities. So I wouldn't be so quick to accuse Unity, unless you include as a "cultist" the apostle Paul. The extant writings of St. Paul contain no references to hell. In three Pauline passages, two Greek words that are sometimes rendered as "hell" actually mean something quite different. In Galatians 1:8-9, Paul twice uses the Greek word *anathema*, which means "accursed" or "consecrated to evil," depending on the context. Considering how angry Paul is at the Galatians for backsliding, there can be no doubt which he meant. Paul also twice employed variations of *apoleia*, which means "destruction," when writing to the Philippians and Thessalonians (Philippians 3:19 and 2 Thessalonians 2:3)— although his authorship of The Second Letter to the Thessalonians is controversial in scholarly circles. Paul apparently believed that sinners who did not confess Jesus as Lord were bound for destruction, that is, extinction of their spiritual existence. *He offered no concept of eternal damnation.* Does that make Pauline Christianity a cult?

Of course, there are ample references to hell in other New Testament books. But as I mentioned in a previous column, these images are the temple furniture of first-century religious thought. Jesus spoke in the metaphors of his day. You'll find nothing about space travel or the Internet in the parables of Jesus because his listeners wouldn't have understood what he was talking about. He told them that resistance to God's goodness can land them in the smoldering ruin of the Jerusalem garbage dump—*gehenna*, in Greek—why, life itself shows us this is true. People create their own hells and refuse to leave.

The most powerful argument against hell can be found in the character of Jesus Christ, who accepted people without behavioral preconditions because he knew that people are capable of growth. That was highly controversial in the ancient world, where people were assumed to have a fixed nature which never changed, cradle to tomb. What possible learning can take place in hell? What goal could eternal punishment achieve, other than to inflict suffering upon creatures who made mistakes in life?

Unity is no cult. We affirm our part of the Christian heritage. But as a Unity minister, I hold that any god who would create a place of eternal torment would be unworthy of worship. Let metaphor be metaphor. Don't force mythology to sit in judgment of gentler insights, gleaned through centuries of growth.

-9-

Holidays and Holy Days

Dear T.M.: Oh, absolutely! I believe in the spirit, imagery and eternal truth behind the nonhistorical metaphors you've listed. Truth is more than historical fact. Sometimes, a good story tells us more truth than any other means. That's why Jesus told stories. Was there a Good Samaritan, a Prodigal Son, a woman who gave her last coin to God? *Does it really matter?*

Dear U.S.: Yes, no, and much, much more. Peace on earth. Planetwide potential. Hope for the species. Humble origins for divine things. Peasants and well-to-do foreigners sharing the vision. Angel choirs and signs in the night sky. All is not as it seems. God is at work behind the scenes. In deep winter, darkest night, under oppression with no relief in sight. Suddenly, the future's bright. No wonder we give presents. It's the birthday of every dream.

Dear Tom: This may not be a spiritual question, but with the Christmas season approaching, I have to ask: What do you think a parent should tell kids about Santa Claus? Is it okay for them to believe in the Jolly Old Elf?

— A.S., Statesboro, Georgia

Dear A.S.: Go for it. A few child psychologists might disagree, but I taught my kids the whole story—the St. Nicholas legend from Asia Minor, Clement Moore's stockings "hung by the chimney with care," Gene Autry singing "Rudolph the Red-Nosed Reindeer"—everything! It's a healthy part of our culture and speaks of generosity, kindness and goodwill.

To keep people focused on the true meaning of the season, some Christian clergy delight in disparaging the secular aspects of religious holidays. For example, take the anti-Santa faction with regard to Christmas, or the anti-colored eggs faction with regard to Easter. But that's just "Grinching" from the pulpit. I made certain my children knew and understood the stories surrounding the birth of Jesus and knew that his nativity will always be "the reason for the season," but what child has been harmed by putting cookies out for Santa?

Dear Tom: How can ministers like you expect children to believe in the Christian faith when you continue to teach fairy tales like a virgin birth, a comet leading Wise Men to the manger of baby Jesus, a census of the Roman world that is not recorded anywhere else, and heavenly choirs serenading terrified shepherds? Doesn't this promote atheism, especially when young people grow up and learn the Christmas myth is no more historical fact than Santa Claus. Call me Scrooge, but I believe children would be better off if we told them the truth.

— **E.S., Boston, Massachusetts**

Dear Mr. Scrooge: Although you correctly point out some problems with the traditional view, the jury of modern biblical scholarship is still deliberating on the historicity of the Nativity. There was no census of the Roman world, but that is merely Luke's device to get Joseph and Mary to Bethlehem, where the Messiah was supposed to be born. If you'll check Matthew's version, no such roll-call tax is mentioned. In fact, these two Gospels are the only biblical sources about the Nativity, and they differ on almost every point in the story. Luke gives us the census, "no room at the inn" and the manger, shepherds and the angel choirs. Matthew reports a house, the Star and the Wise Men. Our traditional Christmas crèche—baby Jesus cradled in straw, angels on the stable roof, shepherds and animals and Wise Men kneeling together, a star hovering above the whole scene—is a composite picture of both Gospels.

Yet, my friend, you miss the point of the Christmas story. *It is a story.* Like any good story, it tells a truth that transcends mere questions about what happened to whom. The Nativity teaches us some important truths about Jesus Christ—that God comes to us in the face of a child; that is, every cradle is a manger and every child the Christ, that all of us are related in some mystical way to God, that wise people will seek Truth and gather with ordinary people (like us shepherds) at the place where Truth is happening.

Try a meditation based on the traditional crèche scene. Move among the baaing sheep and watch the Wise Men open their treasures. Then, take your turn and kneel on the straw, look into the face of this child and hear the angel choirs in the distance. It may not be history, but it is Truth.

Dear Friends: I've been reading a Christmas issue of *Unity Magazine,* in which Thomas Shepherd exposes the "Christmas Myth." The story of Christmas just ain't so; what a shock that will be to those who believe in the Bible. I am left wondering, and I hope Mr. Shepherd will clear this matter up for me: If there were no Wise Men, said to have first consulted King Herod as to where they would find the birthplace of Jesus ... why was Herod called the "slaughterer of the innocents"? Is Herod getting a

bum rap? Please ask Mr. Shepherd to write another column so that we who grew up believing— absolutely—in the biblical account of Jesus' birth can be brought up to speed on what really happened.
— **M.S., New York, New York**

Dear M.S.: I just reread my answer. Here's a quote of the main idea I was trying to convey: "Yet, my friend, you miss the point of the Christmas story. *It is a story.* Like any good story, it tells a truth that transcends mere questions about what happened to whom."

About the historicity issues, here's what the scholarly, Methodist-published, widely circulated, and thoroughly researched *Interpreter's One-Volume Commentary on the Bible* says:

> Herod the king is Herod the Great, who ruled over the Jewish people in Palestine from 37 B.C. to 4 B.C. ... In the course of his reign he arranged the murder of his sons and relatives, as well as of his enemies. The murder of the children is in keeping with his character, although there is no report of this crime from any source other than Matthew.[1]

Not long ago, religious leaders almost succeeded in burning Galileo at the stake for announcing Earth was not the center of the universe. Today we no longer consult ancient authorities for the shape of the cosmos. We expect our astronomers to search the sky and discover what is out there. Likewise, religious scholars dig into Christian history to learn what probably happened. Can Christian Truth really be threatened when those excavations lead to better knowledge?

Dear Tom: When I was a child, I believed Santa Claus loved me and would come every Christmas. I did everything my mom told me, but she said I was a bad little girl so Santa didn't have a present for me. Now, I find out my mom had no extra money. What good is Santa Claus? How can anybody celebrate Christmas when so many little children are poor?
— **H.G., Nashville, Tennessee**

Dear H.G.: Your mom was struggling to make ends meet but chose unfortunate words to tell you there would be no Christmas presents. You were not a "bad little girl." You deserved a happy Christmas even without expensive presents. Lots of parents wrestle with prosperity challenges during the holidays. Simple gifts are always possible.

When I was a boy, my grandmother always dropped an orange in my Christmas stocking. She said it reminded her of the Great Depression, when some families were so destitute they had no food to eat and were living under railroad bridges. To get an out-of-season fruit like an orange for Christmas in those days was a real treat. Although my grandmother's family was never homeless, they were quite poor and saved pennies for months to afford a few oranges for their kids. When Grandmother got her orange, she felt rich.

Prosperity isn't cash in the bank, it's a state of mind that celebrates the good of God's world no matter what is happening around us. A little snip of homemade ribbon, a few inches of aluminum foil, some small gift even if second-hand—why, anybody can give joy and approval at Christmas!

Santa Claus is the perfect symbol for the spirit of Christmas because, like God, Santa approves of everybody. Reports that Santa makes a list of bad boys and girls are myths designed to coerce moral behavior in kids, which seldom works. Most children are too this-minute oriented to worry about what's going to happen in December if they break a family rule today. Besides, we celebrate Christmas because it's a time of unconditional love. Nothing is more important to our poverty-ridden, negative-minded world than a firm belief that everything will work out for the good. You were right. The spirit of love comes to all of us at Christmas, but it isn't in the presents. It's in the season of hope.

May I suggest that you give a gift to that long-ago little girl within you, however belatedly? Go back and see yourself as a child. Tell that disappointed girl that she is not bad, but good. Tell her that God loves and approves of her. Repeat this several times, and then move on to declare that you forgive your mom because she, too, was fighting a difficult battle. Finally, bless all the children in the world; hold them loving-ly in your thoughts. Let the Christ child in you salute the Christ born in every child.

Dear Tom: A local church ran an ad on its billboard that stated: "Santa is Satan." This disturbed a lot of folks, and the minister took the sign down. Why do some people try to spoil holidays? Is it because the celebration doesn't seem religious enough for them?
— **G.W., Martinez, Georgia**

Dear G.W.: Since I was living in your part of the world (Augusta, Georgia) when the ad was published, I read about that incident in the local news. At the risk of offending some of the passionately religious folks in American society, let me reply to those who ran the ad: *Grow up.* You are starting to sound like the Taliban.

Adults should know that all of us, like children, enjoy playtime. Does anyone seriously believe the ghosts and goblins at Halloween are some kind of demonic plot? Can the Thanksgiving turkey be a ploy to lure away the faithful? Do chocolate bunnies and painted eggs mean we don't love Jesus? And Santa—what better testimony points to the goodness of the Christ within than the Saint Nicholas myth? One winter's night, while contemplating the absurdity of this "Santa is Satan" nonsense, I realized that God has a sense of humor, because I could hear divine laughter ringing among the stars.

-10-
Imago Dei

Dear Tom: Jesus cured many people and performed miracles in view of various people. He had disciples and followers. Crowds followed him, as recorded in the Bible. And yet, no one came to His defense at his trial. Why not?
— **J.C., New York City, New York**

Dear J.C.: Human nature. A story I heard years ago about Nikita S. Khrushchev might provide some insight, even if the authenticity of the tale is questionable.[1] During the Russian dictator's reign, he turned against his mentor, the late Joseph Stalin, and blamed "Papa Joe" for all the evils of the communist system. Once when Khrushchev was addressing a huge gathering of workers, railing about "Stalin did this" and "Stalin did that," a voice rang out from the back, saying something like, "Why didn't you denounce Comrade Stalin when it happened, Nikita Sergeyevich? You were there!"

Khrushchev roared back, "Who said that?" And a great silence fell over the multitude. "Now, Comrades," the dictator continued, "you see why I kept silent."

Remember, my friend, it was Jesus alone who had the courage to stand up to the religious and political leaders of his day and proclaim the Truth, because he knew that path lead to Calvary. Many brave people have followed his example. When the test of faith arrives, each of us must ask ourselves the question, "What would Jesus do?" And then, with God's help, do it.

Dear Tom: Do you really believe Jesus Christ rose from the dead?
— **K.R., San Francisco, California**

Dear K.R.: Yes. At least, people closest to him believed he was still alive. There is no doubt among historians that the people who followed Jesus during his lifetime believed they continued to have direct, personal contact with the Risen Lord after his crucifixion. But whether it was a vision, dream or physical appearance, no one can know.

Dear Tom: Do you believe in the virgin birth? Isn't that a relic of paganism?
— **S.C., Seattle, Washington**

Dear S.C.: Sure, its origin is totally pagan. Probably no issue is less relevant or more quibbled over than whether Jesus was born by *parthenogenesis*, that is, asexually, of a virgin. The importance of this doctrine through church history was to reinforce the divinity of Jesus Christ, whose Father was held literally to be God. In the ancient world, heroic figures claimed divine parentage almost matter-of-factly. The Egyptian pharaohs, Achilles, Alexander the Great and the Caesars were all considered sons of the gods.

In the Hellenistic world, establishing the revelatory authority of a cultic figure required a supernatural pedigree. Since most scholars believe that practically nothing is known about Jesus until he showed up at the Jordan River for John's baptism, New Testament authors had free reign to pick the most advantageous story from among the legends circulating about his origin. Even so, only Matthew and Luke mention Mary's virginity, and Matthew's is not clearly a proof-text for parthenogenesis. Luke, however, clearly believed Jesus was supernaturally conceived. The fact that he was writing to a Greek and Roman audience might have had something to do with his inclination toward the miraculous conception. Luke's readers would have yawned and said, "Okay, he was born of a virgin. And your point is …?"

Demythologizing the story and looking at it metaphysically, we see the point is that Jesus was One with God. Just as he was One with the Divine, so are all of us. No miraculous birth is required, for every crib is the manger and every child the Christ. This is the true joy of Christmas: Christ in you, your hope of glory.

Dear Tom: What is the difference between Jesus Christ and the other great teachers of history?
— J.K., Sacramento, California

Dear J.K.: I like to think that Jesus' original contribution to world religious thought was his emphasis on justice and the oneness of humanity. He met with people from all walks of life, Jew and gentile, male and female, and he called them to live their lives based on justice and love. He called them to live the Golden Rule, love their neighbors, love their enemies, return good for evil, forgive everyone, find ways to get along, and go the extra mile. "Blessed are the peacemakers," he said.

To me, Jesus is special because I behold the Christ in him. Jesus Christ shows me what it means to be human and divine. Other messengers of God did this for other communities of faith, but Jesus is the window at which I stand to glimpse the grandeur of the Divine, which some have called "the Christ within." From his manger in Bethlehem to the cross of Calvary, Jesus remains for me the best example of God within us which the human race has yet produced.

There have been other great teachers and prophets, and I honor them, but I joyfully call myself a Christ-ian because at the end of the day when I return to my spiritual home, Jesus the Christ greets me at the door and says all is well.

Dear Tom: I read Marcus Borg's *Meeting Jesus Again for the First Time*, and I liked it. I am wondering whether I am trying to combine apples and oranges here. How does one bridge modern scholarship (theology) and the mystical concepts of Jesus?
— **B.J., South Bend, Indiana**

Imago Dei

Dear B.J.: Apples and oranges work very well in a fruit salad. After some deeper reading, you will probably find that progressive thinkers like John Shelby Spong and Marcus Borg have provided good bridges between mysticism and modern scholarship. In fact, the bulk of mainline Protestant and Catholic scholarship today is quite progressive, especially on the Bible. Religious progressives feel alienated only because the ultraconservatives—the old paradigm people—have succeeded in convincing many that their interpretations of the Christian faith are the authentic Christian faith, which is utter nonsense. Lots of good books discuss this in detail, like Bishop Spong's *Rescuing the Bible From Fundamentalism*. Even better, look into Marcus Borg's more recent book, *The Heart of Christianity*, for a discussion about the old and new paradigms in Christian thought. Highly recommended. Borg will re-lace your walking shoes for the journey ahead.

> **Dear Tom:** How can Jesus be equated to God? Wasn't he just a man? Why is he revered as if he were God?
> **— S.D., Westhampton, New York**

Dear S.D.: I see from the rest of your note that you are a Muslim lady, and I understand how important this question is for people of Muslim and Jewish traditions. To your specific question—for me, Jesus was not just a man. He was the Divine incarnate. But whereas most Christian theologies stop there, making Jesus the unique Son of God, metaphysical Christianity continues up the mountain to discover the Divine dwelling within everyone. Like any wise traveler would follow a competent guide, we follow him because Jesus shows us the way to see the Divine within ourselves. His birth, life, teachings, death and resurrection define God's nature for us, so that our God concept is in reality a Jesus concept. The fourth Gospel records this remarkable passage:

> Jesus answered, "Is it not written in your law, 'I said, you are gods'? If those to whom the word of God came were called 'gods'—and the scripture cannot be annulled—can you say that the one whom the Father has sanctified and sent into the world is blaspheming because I said, 'I am God's Son'?"[2]

Although this idea works for me, it probably will not speak to the Islamic experience. But I never intended to convert you anyway, just to share some ideas between us fellow mountain climbers.

-11-

The Bible for Postmodern Skeptics

Dear Tom: I have prayed and pondered about one certain phrase in the 23rd Psalm: "Thou preparest a table before me in the presence of mine enemies" (Psalm 23:5 KJV). For some reason, I really don't understand what this means. What table, what enemies? Please enlighten me about this, so that I may stop going back over and over this, trying to figure it out.

— **H.C.W., Tulsa, Oklahoma**

Dear H.C.W.: The simplest explanation is often the best. The psalmist was talking to a warlike people who had enemies. When they were able to sit down and eat a meal, even besieged by an enemy army, it meant they had abundant prosperity.

However, metaphysical interpretation always sees biblical passages as metaphors for the process of spiritual growth. So let's do a metaphysical interpretation of this passage. Today enemies come in subtler form. Can you affirm your divine right to prosperity when confronted by unemployment, when surrounded by hosts of naysayers who shout negative thoughts at you, or when the walls of your Truth citadel are assailed by self-doubts? If so, divine order stands ready to anoint your head with kingly oil and pour out overflowing measure of abundance into your cup. (Key point: Don't worry about passages you can't understand. Maybe you aren't ready yet.)

Dear Tom: Since I have been reading the Bible more, I have noticed that some translations use the word *life* instead of *soul* in Mark 8:36, 37. For me, the word *life* changes the whole meaning of the verses. How does the average person fight this? It's hard for me to accept these new versions.
— **K.K., San Francisco, California**

Dear K.K.: You share the feelings of many who are frustrated with the changes to the Bible, which probably started when lots of new translations began appearing in the 1960s. Folks who grew up with a steady diet of the King James or Revised Standard versions sometimes experienced the sourness of unfamiliar wording in the newer editions.

However, the Bible isn't a *version*. In reality, it's a mass of ancient manuscripts that have been screened countless times since the long-lost originals were penned. Modern biblical scholarship begins by examining the manuscripts that have survived from antiquity and comparing their variant readings, because there are many, many variations on every page of Scripture. So when the New English Bible or Today's

English Version translates a word or phrase, it might sound different to our KJV or RSV-trained ears. The translator's job is to render faithfully the ancient text into whatever language the reader requires to comprehend the message of the author.

The Greek word used in Mark 8:36, 37 (*psuche*) usually means *life*, but it can refer to more than just life of the physical body. The exhaustive, authoritative reference book *A Greek-English Lexicon of the New Testament and Other Early Christian Literature,* says *psuche* can also refer to "the soul as seat and center of life that transcends the earthly" and specifically mentions the Marcan passages. For some reason, most modern translators have chosen to ignore this meaning and have rendered *psuche* in its simplest terms, meaning "life" itself. But we know that life is more than just the physical realm. Life is eternal. In this sense, both translations work. Meditate on the words *soul* and *life* and see how inseparable they are.

Dear Tom: I've always wondered about the quotation "Ye shall know the truth, and the truth shall make you free." Just what is this truth we should know?
— **A.B., La Mirada, California**

Dear A.B.: The passage comes from the book of John, but you quoted only the last half in the King James. Here's the whole text from the New Revised Standard Version:

> Then Jesus said to the Jews who had believed in
> him, "If you continue in my word, you are truly
> my disciples; and you will know the truth, and
> the truth will make you free."[1]

Two millennia have passed since those words were written, and countless millions have found a truth that sets them
free in the life, teachings, death and resurrection of Jesus.
There may be other truths that set people free, but surely the
message of Jesus has demonstrated its liberating power
through the ages.

Dear Tom: Why is it the apostle Paul never told any
stories about Jesus? He lived at the same time; surely, he knew events in the Master's life. What about
the parables, or the Sermon on the Mount, or the
loaves and fishes? Whether you read about Paul in
Acts or look at his letters, you find a lot of Christ
and very little Jesus. Why?
— **T.Q., Denver, Colorado**

Dear T.Q.: Excellent question, and very insightful.
Apparently, Paul tells only one "story" about Jesus in the
seven undisputed Pauline letters. It is his brief description of
the Last Supper in 1 Corinthians 11:23-26. And although the
Paul we meet in Acts is Luke's literary character and not the
historic Saul of Tarsus, even Luke's Paul tells little of Jesus'
earthly life—not a parable, not an incident, not a story.

There are several possible reasons for this. First, he wasn't there during the years when Jesus wandered with the disciples, so Paul may not have been able to speak with authority about those times. Also, Paul is more interested in "Christ Jesus" (his preferred word for the risen Lord) than the earthly Jesus of Nazareth. Less charitably, one might speculate that the apostle to the gentiles simply didn't know the details of Jesus' life as a Palestinian Jew, and because of his emphasis on the post-Resurrection Lord, Paul never took the time to learn the stories and saying floating around the Jewish Christian community.

Besides, telling the Jesus stories was the teaching province of eyewitnesses like Peter, James and John. Gospel writers like Mark, Luke and Matthew came later, after most of the first generation had died as martyrs. Following their work would be theologians like the unknown authors of John; Deutero-Pauline works like Ephesians, Hebrews, Colossians and the so-called "pastoral letters" like Titus and Timothy; and wildly speculative books like Revelation, which was the lone example of that genre to make it into the New Testament canon.

Each New Testament author pursues his goals and employs the tools that will make his point. For Paul, the historical Jesus only serves as a staging area to launch the risen Christ into the heavens. He is utterly committed to faith in the resurrected Lord as the path to salvation. Paul is less concerned with stories and more with doctrine, because he believed it was through right thinking that a person would be transformed.

Of course, Christians today can agree with this premise without necessarily accepting his formula for achieving it. Most people find the Jesus stories to be enlightening and revelatory. For me, they show Jesus as kinetic divinity, God in motion, and illustrate how the human-divine paradox within each person can transcend its limits and become the Christ. Since he was also fully human, his accomplishment awaits our efforts to become reality in our lives too.

Dear Tom: I'm reading your articles in the German version of *Unity Magazine,* and I would like to ask for your help in understanding the Revelation of John. What do the angels with the seven trumpets and the apocalypse have to do with an all-loving God? I would be grateful for your answer and wish you God's blessings for your work.

— J.H., Hennef-Sieg, Germany

Dear J.H.: The Revelation to John is a fiercely symbolic work. Because Revelation is steeped in the events and issues of the late first century C.E., modern readers are easily lost in its labyrinth of symbolism. However, the basic message is clear and simple: *Don't worship the Beast. The end is near. Be faithful, even under threat of death, and you will receive spiritual rewards beyond measure.* The book was probably written for underground Christian communities during times of persecution; the people understood that "the Beast" meant Roman power.

What is the lasting power of this series of wild visions? Why has every generation since the ink first dried on the original autographs believed its phantasmagoric prophecies were coming true in their times? Simply because every generation faces its inevitable end in physical death, and every generation must decide whether to worship its particular Beast or to serve the God of compassionate love.

If you'd like more information on the symbolism of Revelation, I'm certain there are excellent publications on the subject in German by Protestant and Catholic scholars. Also, to get a great overview of the Bible, try Rudolf Bultmann's revolutionary essay *The New Testament and Mythology*, written originally in German. If you do a Google search, you can probably find an online version of Bultmann's 1940 essay, which is available in English as well as German.

Dear Tom: I have been given the task of discovering the meaning of verse 11 in Chapter 1 of the Letter of Jude in the New Testament. It is very complicated, because it talks about the "way of Cain" and "running after the error of Balaam," both of which had easily discoverable explanations in Charles Fillmore's Metaphysical Bible Dictionary. My question is, Can you send me material or uncover the meaning of the word *Cor'-e*? My instincts tell me it has something to do with attempting to gain the "core of substance" (the central heart of God, for

lack of a better term) the easy way—by attempting to "find God" without putting in the hard work. I'd be interested in your thoughts.
— **C.W., New Zealand**

Dear C.W.: Blessings to our Unity friends in New Zealand! Lovely to hear from you, but I have to confess—I've been in the ministry over 30 years, and I don't think I've ever meditated on the Letter of Jude, not to mention the word *Core* or *Korah*. Taking a quick look at the *Interpreter's One-Volume Commentary on the Bible*, it seems *Korah* was a character in the Hebrew Scriptures, mentioned in Numbers 16, with whom Moses had a power struggle. The *IOVC* says: "Basically, all three (Cain, Balaam and Korah) are examples of the danger which the author of Jude saw as the rejection of the way of God and the indulgence in self-seeking."[2] So if this interpretation is correct, Korah could represent those who chase spiritual fads and neglect the central matters of faith, hope and love. Your guess is as good as anybody's.

Frankly, these obscure texts can be interpreted as saying anything the creative interpreter wants to hear. Next time, try Paul's Letter to the Philippians. I've actually read that one, and it's really good.

Dear Tom: In view of the fact that on so many occasions Jesus of Nazareth taught that "the kingdom is within," which I take to mean that God is within, why on occasion did he gesture to God, Abba or

Father outside himself? An example is in Mark 6:41: "Taking the five loaves and the two fish, he looked up to heaven." Where did he look? Could it be that Jesus truly was a master psychologist teaching to the audience of that time?
— P.G., Miami, Florida

Dear P.G.: Do you really want to say God is *not* up there when lifting your eyes heavenward? Of course, there is no physical heaven teeming with gods and angels in the clouds over head. That is a remnant of the ancient, flat-earth, three-story universe. Many spiritual writings address the *impersonal* nature of the Divine. However, we can push this metaphysical subtlety too far. To say that God is *impersonal* doesn't mean God is *less than* personal. Perhaps God is best understood as *transpersonal*, which includes both the impersonal and personal and goes way beyond either viewpoint. The Bible simply declares that God is love, and that's about as personal as you can get.

Actually if God is not out there, we have a deeper problem. Insisting that God is strictly within makes God a subjective experience, not an eternal reality. Alfred North Whitehead, one of the most profound philosophers of the 20th century, observed:

> God is in the world, or nowhere, creating continually in us and around us. This creative principle is everywhere, in animate and so-called inanimate matter, in the ether, water, earth, human hearts. But this creation is a continuing process,

and the "the process is itself the actuality," since no sooner do you arrive than you start on a fresh journey. Insofar as man partakes of this creative process does he partake of the divine, of God, and that participation is his immortality, reducing the question of whether his individuality survives death of the body to the estate of an irrelevancy. His true destiny as co-creator in the universe is his dignity and his grandeur.[3]

The Missouri mystic, Charles Fillmore, added in *Keep a True Lent*: "God as principle is the absolute good expressed in all creation." Of course, God the Absolute Good is within us, but that doesn't mean God isn't out there too. One Presence and One Power is everywhere, equally distributed in all creation.

I think it's a bit anachronistic to think of Jesus as a psychologist, considering the ideas of Freud and Jung were many centuries in the future. A good showman? Maybe. A historian might suggest that Jesus looked up to heaven because that's where Yahweh, the sky god worshipped as supreme by ancient Israel, lived. And in the spirit of theological diversity let me confess that in times of need I still do it, murmuring, "Lord, help me!" as I pray to the god of the ceiling. There's nothing wrong with seeing God out there as long as we realize God is best found *in here*. To paraphrase Whitehead: Creation is a continuing process ... as we partake of this creative process, we partake of the divine, of God, and that participation is our immortality. Our true destiny as co-creator in the universe is our dignity and our grandeur.

Dear Tom: There is a scripture in Matthew 7:9-11 which has always troubled me regardless of how it is interpreted. It reads, "Is there anyone among you who, if your child asks for bread, will give a stone? Or if the child asks for a fish, will give a snake? If you then, who are evil, know how to give good gifts to your children, how much more will your Father in heaven give good things to those who ask him!" The phrase I have problems with and would like interpreted is, "If you then, who are evil ...." If you have a book or books you would recommend to assist in interpretation of Scriptures metaphysically, I would like to receive your suggestions.

— J.L.W., via Internet

Dear J.L.W.: In the verse you cited, the word translated "evil" is the Greek term *poneros*, which primarily means "full of labors, annoyances and hardships." It also has a secondary meaning of "physical malady," such as blindness or disease. Third, an ethical component can be present, "wickedness." However, the context does not require this last interpretation but suggests any sort of limitation would do. So why not translate the passage: "If you, *who are imperfect*, know how to give good gifts to your children ..."?

Also note the verse directly following (7:12) is the Golden Rule. If we were inherently evil, the rule would be impossible to keep.

Good Questions

-12-

Lost Books, Lost Years—Found Now

> Dear Tom: I have in my possession a copy of *The Lost Books of the Bible,* in which there are chapters about the years of Jesus' youth, presumably available with other manuscripts used informing our present-day Bible. The decision as to which documents to include in our Bible was apparently in the hands of a few appointed men who, in effect, tailormade the Christian faith and presented Jesus as the man who knew no sin. The accounts of his deeds in youthful years present a picture of a vengeful young man. I have long carried these doubts ... can you help?
>
> **— H.C., Orlando, Florida**

Dear H.C.: When people discover these "lost" books, they often think there is some grand conspiracy afoot here. I actually heard a nationally known author perpetuating this urban legend by accusing the Catholic Church of gathering in some secret enclave and ripping these books from the Bible. Historically speaking, that is utter nonsense. By the time the early medieval Church began drafting lists of the books that were supposed to constitute the New Testament, the decision had already been made by popular demand. Even so, these books were not lost at all. There are two editions of the volume you reference, on the shelf of my rather small personal library.

Several Jewish and Christian books fit this "lost books" genre. The Christian books are called the New Testament *Apocrypha* ("things hidden"). Although falsely claiming to be the work of original apostles, these books were written sometime after the second century A.D. They were utterly rejected by the young church for many reasons, including elements you cited: the picture of Jesus drawn in several of the books is mean and vengeful.

But these books weren't ruled out by a council of gray-bearded celibates who wanted to cover up scandals in the life of Jesus. They were simply ignored by the vast majority of believing Christians—clergy and laity alike—because the quality of their spiritual teaching generally did not measure up to the ethical and spiritual standard of the books that made it into the New Testament canon (the Church's official library). I recommend the excellent article on the New Testament Apocrypha in Volume One of *The Interpreter's Dictionary of the Bible*, from which I quote: "The unfortunate impression that these books were suppressed by the same imaginary group who determined the Christian canon, has been heightened by the utterly unjustified claims made for other volumes of modern apocrypha, such as the so-called *[The] Lost Books of the Bible*."[1]

If you want to learn about Jesus, go to the closest sources: read the seven authentic letters of Paul (which are the oldest

New Testament works) and The Gospel According to Mark (which is the oldest Gospel). You won't find Jesus spiteful in those pages, but human and compassionate, divine and life-affirming in his proclamation of Truth. Our ancestors in the faith knew what they were doing when common folk, not high councils of the clergy, selected the canonical books of the Bible through common use.

Dear Tom: I would be interested in your thoughts about the Lost Gospels and the idea that there were many Gospels that were suppressed. Do you think that this was done to discount the role of Mary Magdalene and other women in the early church? Can you recommend any books or articles on this topic?
— **M.S., Concord, California**

Dear M.S.: As much as I'd like to help the women's movement, historical facts don't lend support to your theory. *The DaVinci Code*, which prompted a flash-flood of discussion on this topic, is a well-researched work of fiction. However, neither semipagan Constantine nor the celibate church fathers decided alone which books would make it into the biblical canon. Books made it into the Bible by popular demand and common usage, not by decrees from church or state officials. To "preserve" a biblical book meant to copy it by hand, an expensive and meticulous process which was not wasted on literature that people didn't find appealing. Many of the "lost" books were so deviant from the mainstream of Christian thought that the people of the wider church rejected them.

Canonical New Testament books, that is, the works which were eventually accepted as sacred Scripture, were written in approximately a 100-year period from the 50s of the first century to the year 150 C.E. First Thessalonians was probably the earliest, Second Peter was apparently last. Also, a lot of books and letters began appearing in the second century which claimed to come from the earlier times, the days of the apostles. These are patent forgeries, generally quite different in tone and theology from the books that eventually made up the canon. They are uneven in content, as even a cursory reading will disclose. Some were full of high spiritual content, like the Didache and the Shepherd of Hermas, while others were problematic at best. Some books were downright zany, others angry or violent, and still others were simply flights of fantasy, but all were written with theological agendas. The authors tried to validate their opinions and speculative theories by claiming the books were written by apostles or other respected figures.

We can usually find ideas in any spiritual work that seem friendly enough, but the overall tone of the composition must be considered, not just a text here or there. For example, the much-touted Gospel of Thomas contains some exquisite passages and previously unknown "sayings" of Jesus. However good the text may be in places, the Gospel of Thomas proceeds from a dualistic Gnostic point of view. For example, the Coptic version of the Gospel of Thomas ends with this un-Jesus-like denigration of all females past, present and future:

Simon Peter said to him, "Let Mary leave us, for women are not worthy of Life." Jesus said, "I myself shall lead her in order to make her male, so that she too may become a living spirit resembling you males. For every woman who will make herself male will enter the Kingdom of Heaven."[2]

That hardly sounds like Gloria Steinem. Gnosticism, with its world-denying dualism and fear of anything pleasurable, runs rampant in the noncanonical books. And if you want a terrifying portrait of Jesus as a youth, check out the Infancy Narratives, in which little Jesus kills a boy who strikes him. The text says Jesus curses him, "and immediately he fell to the earth and died" (Infancy Gospel of Thomas, Latin text, 5:1).

My point is this: Sample the content of these noncanonical books, then do a little reading in the New Testament. The people in the early Church knew what they were doing when they preserved the Sermon on the Mount and rejected the Gnostic view of this world as a place of evil. After a while, a consensus developed about which books belonged in the Bible and which were—well, a little flaky. Church officials could not have kept the widely dispersed and independently functioning scribes and copyists from producing New Testaments if they had tried.

Dear Tom: Why doesn't the Bible address Jesus' life when he was 15 to 25 years old? Where was he then? Isn't this a relevant time?
— **T.B., Augusta, Georgia**

Dear T.B.: I suspect the Bible doesn't mention the so-called "lost years" of Jesus because it isn't terribly important. Nevertheless, plenty of modern books have been written about young man Jesus. I've heard he went to India or spent his adolescence with Egyptian mystics. A favorite "lost years" destination for Jesus is the Essene community, perhaps at Qumran to help those Jewish monks copy the Dead Sea Scrolls. This is pure speculation, based on the idea that Jesus could never become spiritually attuned and one with God while driving nails in a carpenter shop in Nazareth! He must have studied with the mystic masters. Actually, he did just that. He studied with the Master Teacher, the divine Spirit within him. It's too easy to say that "Jesus had special help ... he was somehow different ... he got extra training unavailable to me."

As we used to say during the 1960s, *that's a cop-out*. If Jesus could become One with God while sawing lumber in a mud-brick house in a Galilean village, then nobody has a legitimate excuse for delaying spiritual growth. He did it in an everyday locale; so can we. Away with the Cinderella notion that someone will sweep us off to enlightenment by blessing us with special knowledge.

The most likely answer is the least romantic—he probably spent it working in his father's carpentry shop in Galilee. Studying with a guru is, in Unity's teaching, unnecessary.

None of us needs exalted spiritual teachers to link with the Divine, since God is within each of us in equal measure. We need time to practice the Presence, and that can happen anywhere. The flip side of this likely historical scenario is this: If Jesus could get all he needed to be one with the Father while sawing timber and driving nails, so can we unfold our magnificent spiritual natures in the humdrum of everyday life.

Dear Tom: What credibility is there to the Eastern scriptures and histories that place Jesus in the Far East during the so-called lost years, which have been so neatly excised from our Scriptures?
— **T.Y. (a fellow University of Idaho Vandal; no city provided)**

Dear Brother Vandal: Whenever I hear this question, I'm moved to ask, "What lost years?" The Gospel of Luke tells exactly what happened:

> Now every year his parents went to Jerusalem for the festival of the Passover. And when he was twelve years old, they went up as usual for the festival.... Then he went down with them and came to Nazareth, and was obedient to them. His mother treasured all these things in her heart. And Jesus increased in wisdom and in years, and in divine and human favor (Luke 2:41-42, 51-52, NRSV).

Historical point of order: No passages supporting a *Young Indiana Jones* phase of Jesus' life have been excised from Christian Scripture. Long after Christianity was firmly established, sometime in the second and third centuries C.E., speculative books were written and backdated to the apostolic age. Some of these books dealt with allegedly missing time spans in Jesus' life. These works are transparent attempts by later groups to slip their beliefs into the mainstream by claiming divine authority through the vehicle of apostolic authorship.

In that regard, they are not unlike *A Course in Miracles*, which makes the rather silly claim of being dictated by Jesus himself. As with *A Course in Miracles*, you can read the so-called lost and forgotten books of the Bible today. Decide for yourself. Frankly, I'm not always certain I'm hearing the authentic, historical Jesus in the four canonical Gospels, let alone in *A Course in Miracles* or the Infancy Narratives.

-13-

Parables and Assorted Goodies

Dear Tom: I've been a Holy Ghost-filled minister of music for half my 72 years, but there is one scripture that puzzles me to this day. Jesus curses the fig tree which was not in season for figs, and the tree withers. This makes Jesus sound like he is having a temper tantrum, and this is not the Jesus I know.
— **K.N., El Cerrito, California**

Dear K.N.: If you regard the story as a historical event, there are definitely some ethical problems here for most Christians. But if it represents the testimony of the early Church that Jesus had mastery over the forces of his world—to include nature—then the story can be seen as it was probably intended, that is, as just another testimony to his special mission from the Divine, an incident comparable to Jesus stilling the storm at sea. The fig tree is a fable which attempts to show the power of Jesus over the physical universe; it's not an ethical lesson about what was fair to the tree. I doubt the author of the tale, who lived long before the environmentally conscious era of today, would even understand why you are upset. I can hear him shouting, *"Hey, man, it's only a tree!"*

Think parable. Literature, not history.

Dear Tom: What is your interpretation of Jesus' parable of the householder who paid the same wages to the laborers who worked all day and those who worked for a short time? Please explain, "So the last shall be first, and the first last: for many be called, but few chosen" (Matthew 20:16 KJV).
— **L.R., Jupiter, Florida**

Dear L.R.: Many biblical interpreters agree with you that this parable is one of the most difficult of Jesus' sayings to interpret for modern readers. According to one weighty source— the massive, yet highly readable, *Interpreter's One-Volume Commentary on the Bible*—the verse you quote in your letter might have been appended to the parable by mistake, since it seems to change the meaning of the story. The workers were all paid the same wages, regardless of how long they worked in the fields, so the last and the first were all equal, not ranked in status or reward.[1]

The last half of the verse (many called/few chosen) is not present in the oldest manuscripts and is generally omitted in modern translations. Furthermore, New Testament scholar Howard Clark Kee says the key verse is not the one you quoted but the comments of the householder immediately preceding it: "Am I not allowed to do what I choose with what belongs to me? Or do you begrudge my generosity?" (Matthew 20:15 RSV). Kee writes: "The central actor is the generous householder, not the disgruntled employees. The parable is a defense of Jesus' message of God's grace to all."[2]

In truth, we know that God loves us equally, regardless of how hard we "work" at our spiritual growth. The greatest benefit of working in the "Lord's vineyard" is not found in the wages we receive but rather in the labor itself. Spiritual growth is its own reward. Besides, any other attitude is a poverty consciousness, not a faithful reliance on Divine Supply. If the daylong laborers had cheerfully accepted their blessing of prosperity the way the hour-long workers did, who knows what extraordinary bounties might have deluged their lives?

> Dear Tom: I want to know about the bizarre parable Jesus told in Matthew 12:43-45. I've never heard a sermon on this. Can you make any sense of it?
> — C.A., Carmel, California

Dear C.A.: Oh, yeah. You're absolutely right. Matthew 12:43-45 is one of the nuttiest parables in the Bible. At first reading, it sounds like a case of demonic forces overwhelming an innocent soul. It's also possible to see the characters, places and events in biblical stories as symbolizing the growth of the individual soul, so that everything happens within us. When people drive out an "evil spirit"—whether a self-destructive habit like alcoholism, drug abuse or overeating or a self-defeating attitude like fear, hate or jealousy—they are also creating a new space in their lives. Someone tries to maintain this empty space; it can quickly fill with something else, perhaps something even more undesirable. Reformed alcoholics sometimes smoke themselves to emphysema; former drug addicts may begin heavy drinking; newly slim overeaters could gain the weight back and more.

What recovering people need is to replace the "evil spirit" with something good. Drive out the demon of self-hate, and replace it with a new self-image that knows you are a child of God. Give up abusing alcohol or drugs, and get involved with helping others do the same, the AA solution. Lose weight, and take up tennis, hiking or aerobic dancing. When the "demon" returns, your house will have a "no vacancy" sign, and the demon will return to the "waterless regions."

Dear Tom: In all my 80 years I have never heard anyone make a suggestion as to what Jesus wrote in the sand during the incident of the woman caught in adultery. Could you please tell me what your answer or interpretation is?
— M.L., Ft. Lauderdale, Florida

Dear M.L.: You are referring to the passage in John 8:2-11, particularly verses 6-9:

Jesus bent down and wrote with his finger on the ground. When they kept on questioning him, he straightened up and said to them, "Let anyone among you who is without sin be the first to throw a stone at her." And once again he bent down and wrote on the ground. When they heard it, they went away, one by one, beginning with the elders; and Jesus was left alone with the woman standing before him.

There are some serious historical questions about the authenticity of this passage, which doesn't even appear in the oldest known manuscripts. I like to think of the "Woman Caught in the Act of Adultery" as a parable about the life of Jesus. Even taking it literally, there really is no way to know what he wrote. However, several scholars have played with various ideas about the scribbling of Jesus. One provocative but highly speculative idea is that Jesus listed some common given names of Jewish girls. Since most of the men in the crowd were guilty of the very offense the woman had been caught doing, the names of women struck terror in their hearts. One can almost hear them thinking, "Does this accursed carpenter really know about me and the shoe-maker's wife?" And the older ones dropped their stones first.

Perhaps the real answer is less colorful. For example, the author of the Book of John may not tell us because it isn't important. Jesus wrote in the dirt to take himself out of the action while the crowd mulled their options. It is his refusal to judge a person's worth by their current behavior that distinguishes Jesus from the mob. He knew that Divine Spirit dwelled within the woman caught in adultery, and in each of her accusers too. He called everyone to a higher consciousness of divine forgiveness and omnipresent love.

Dear Tom: I have always had a problem with the portion of the Lord's Prayer that reads, "And lead us not into temptation ..." How can God, who is altogether good, possibly lead us into temptation? I have heard this interpreted, "Try us not, O God, beyond our level of spiritual understanding." If this is true, why doesn't our prayer say so more directly?

— **K.S., Carmichael, California**

Dear K.S.: Read on.

Dear Tom: I have been visiting several churches in Florida. Much to my dismay, some are altering the Lord's Prayer. They are changing the word "evil" to "error." It's one thing to teach interpretation; it's another to change it.

— **R.W., Clearwater, Florida**

Dear K.S. and R.W.: I'd love to hear you two discuss this one! I like both the interpretations you've mentioned (evil = error; try us not beyond our level ...). Good interpretation of Scripture is always controversial, especially if your theology awards the Bible a strong place of authority. If the written Word has the force of divine law, the battle over what is the "correct" interpretation becomes a bloody fight for the high ground. Most progressive churches combine historical analysis and common sense when interpreting the Bible, and virtually all mainline Protestant/Catholic scholars begin with the assumption that *people* wrote the Scriptures from differing perspectives.

Now, about interpretation vs. changing the text—a lot of this is going on today. Politically correct translations abound. There's nothing new about this. I agree with the conservatives on this issue. The most important principle in translating the biblical writings is to render their original Hebrew and Greek forms into modern English as accurately as possible, regardless of whether we like the results. If this causes problem passages, so be it. That's why we have theologians, ministers, teachers and discussion groups. You don't win the game by changing the rules at halftime. Where I come from, that's called something other than interpretation.

Having said that, let me suggest that a *paraphrase* for personal reflection is okay, unless one insists the creative rewording is somehow a better rendition of the original text, which it probably is not. Paraphrasing is not translation, but a restatement of main ideas in different ways. Sometimes paraphrasing promotes deeper reflection. Charles Fillmore's well-known paraphrase of the passage—"Leave us not in temptation"—is a good example of what I am describing.

Even though I would not change the text when reading or singing it, self-conscious paraphrasing, to find other possible meanings to meditate upon, certainly can be helpful. Let me add my own paraphrase to the discussion: Instead of "Lead us not in to temptation …," why not hear the author praying for God to "Lead us away from temptation …"? Do you have a creative paraphrase that works for you?

Dear Tom: In my Bible the Lord's Prayer ends with "deliver us from evil." When we say or sing it, we always add: "For Thine is the Kingdom, and the Power, and the Glory, forever. Amen." Why?
— **M.L.F.H., Harrisonburg, Virginia**

Dear M.L.F.H.: That is a very good question, one I'd never considered before your letter. At first, I thought that Roman Catholics recited the shorter version and that I'd have to research why Protestants keep on praying after the biblical version ends. Then I discovered that after Vatican II, Catholics joined the Protestants in adding "For thine is the Kingdom ..." to the Lord's Prayer when said as part of the Mass. Protestants were already saying the prayer with this doxology tacked to the end ... but why? Because, although the best ancient manuscripts omit the last phrase, the longer version is found in the King James Version of the Bible, which for nearly four centuries has been the most popular Bible in the world. You might also check out the other, even shorter version of the Lord's Prayer found in Luke 11:2-4. And if you can get a copy of the Didache, the second century book also known as the *Teaching of the Apostles*, you'll find this version:

> Our Father, which art in heaven,
> hallowed be Thy name;
> Thy kingdom come;
> Thy will be done,
> as in heaven, so also on earth;
> give us this day our daily bread
> and forgive us our debt,

as we forgive our debtors;
and lead us not into temptation,
but deliver us from the evil one;
for Thine is the power and the glory
for ever and ever.[3]

Sound familiar? Finally, here's what Emmet Fox
(1886–1951) said about this great prayer:

> The more one analyzes the Lord's Prayer, the
> more wonderful is its construction seen to be. It
> meets everyone's need just at his own level. It not
> only provides a rapid spiritual development for
> those who are sufficiently advanced to be ready,
> but in its superficial meaning it supplies the more
> simpleminded and even the more materially
> minded people with just what they need at the
> moment, if they use the prayer sincerely.[4]

Dear Tom: I am married to a very adulterous man. I
have caught him in the act of adultery, and since
our marriage of 12 years began, he has had a child
by each of two other women. I know the Bible says
Jesus wants us to forgive seven times 70 and that
love does not keep a count of wrongdoing. I have
also heard that in the Old Testament you could give
a person a written notice of divorce, but Jesus
doesn't accept divorce. My questions are these:

1. When do you stop being a Christian and start being a fool?
2. Where is it in the Bible that Jesus does not agree with a divorce?
3. When Paul was describing love as suffering long and bearing all things; did he have someone like my husband in mind?
— **L.A., Athens, Georgia**

Dear L.A.: *Run*, do not walk, away from this man. God does not require you to submit yourself to mistreatment. Forgive him, but move on. In a case like yours, Jesus would type the divorce papers himself. The sole exception he made was designed for cases like yours. Jesus allows divorce for unfaithfulness, and it sounds like your husband qualifies for the exemption.

> It was also said, "Whoever divorces his wife, let him give her a certificate of divorce." But I say to you that anyone who divorces his wife, except on the ground of unchastity, causes her to commit adultery; and whoever marries a divorced woman commits adultery.[5]

In a broader interpretation of Scripture, we have to note that the no-divorce rule made sense in the ancient world, where there was no social safety net with court-enforced child support payments. A woman summarily "dumped" could crawl back to the charity of her family or seek the sole occupation readily available to women throughout the ages.

Neither of these options was satisfactory to Jesus, who forbade breakups in order to protect women and their children. Today social conditions have changed, but the basic spiritual teaching is still valid—marriage should be forever, covenants must be honored, but mitigating circumstances can force people to make painful, necessary choices. To stay with this man exposes you to HIV infection and other sexually transmitted diseases, not to mention the impact it must have on your children. You've suffered long enough. Move on, and don't look back.

> Dear Tom: Is there much said about Joseph, the father of Jesus, in the Bible?
> — **M.P., Reading, Pennsylvania**

Dear M.P.: Blessings to you and everyone who lives in and around my home town of Reading (pronounced "Redding"). To answer your inquiry about Joseph, not much is known about him. Joseph is specifically mentioned 21 times, all confined to the opening chapters of Matthew, Luke and John. Mark, thought to be the oldest Gospel, is silent about Jesus' birth and childhood. There is also the vague reference to Jesus' parents who returned to find him in the Temple when the boy was 12 years old. Luke and John report that the people knew of Joseph, and it fueled the grumbling about Jesus as a country hick from Galilee (Luke 4:22, John 6:42). There are some ancient works that purport to tell complex tales about the life of Jesus, including incidents with his father and mother, but these books were rightly rejected by early

Christians as pure fiction, the tabloid editions of postbiblical paparazzi. The fact is, we know little or nothing about Jesus before he was baptized by John, so accurate information about his immediate family is unavailable.

Metaphysically, however, Joseph and Mary represent wisdom and love. They illustrate the best of human consciousness, that which obeys the Divine within and follows God's guidance regardless of appearances to the contrary. Together they work to bring forth the divine nature (Christ) in every human being. Today Joseph is popular as the patron saint of caregivers. All of my brothers and sisters were born at St. Joseph's Hospital in Reading, Pennsylvania.

Dear Tom: Since the Bible has a "fire and brimstone" old section and the newer, softer New Testament, what if anything is Jesus alleged to have said about homosexuality and gay marriage? While I'm on the topic, some of my gay friends have told me there is ample evidence that Paul was homosexual. Is there any scholarly research to support this idea, or is it purely an urban legend?
— **G.B., San Diego, California**

Dear G.B.: I understand your sentiment, but take another look at the Bible. You have rather unfairly characterized the Jewish Scriptures as being more violent and judgmental than the New Testament. May I suggest a casual reading of the Book of Revelation, with its epoch-shattering, earth-melting war between good and evil, lake of fire, stars falling and so forth? It makes Joshua's battle of Jericho look like a game of dodge ball. Of course, what we have throughout the Bible is legend, myth, story, parable, praise, prayer and hymnody, with a dash of history to hold the whole mess together.

That's the formula for much of the religious literature of the planet; why would it be different for our Christian heritage? The Bible is the book of memories; it tells us who we are and points to the magnificent and the lowly in human character. Shadow and bright sunlight, all are here. St. Paul is an example of these contradictory tendencies in Scripture. Sometimes he is massively inspirational, as in 1 Corinthians 13. In other passages he comes off as petty and mean-spirited. He was one of us, struggling to understand what it all meant and to make his insights available to others. We owe him the right to be heard even when we don't agree with him—even when he is patently absurd. We can learn from mistakes as well as from success. (Look at King David!)

There is actually some debate in both scholarly and popular literature about Paul's sexual preferences. No less a figure than Bishop John Shelby Spong believes the apostle to the gentiles was gay. Internet authors Matt and Andrej Koymasky summarize the pro-gay-Paul argument at their Web site:

> The fact he was never married, unusual for a Jew of his time, his companionship with a series of younger men, especially St. Timothy, his mention of an unnamed "thorn in the flesh," and, possibly, his disdain for some types of exploitative homosexual relationship in his period all raise

questions, which cannot be answered it must be admitted, about his sexuality.[6]

I'm not convinced either way, and absent any strong evidence I think we should assume Paul was straight, with a typical first-century Jewish attitude toward homosexuality, in other words, that it was an abomination. "Do not fool yourselves; people who are immoral or who worship idols or are adulterers or homosexual perverts or who steal or are greedy or are drunkards or who slander others or are thieves—none of these will possess God's Kingdom" (1 Corinthians 6:9-10, TEV). Please note: I am not suggesting Paul was speaking eternal truths here. As well as being a gay-basher, Paul shared the ancient world's male-dominant attitude toward women. He never condemned the institution of slavery either. Social conditions change as the times change; spiritual Truths are forever true. This is why we look for the principle behind the particular.

I can summarize what Jesus said about homosexuality and gay marriage in one word: nothing. He never mentions it. If the matter were so pressing, you'd think Jesus might have thrown a "woe to ye" in there while excoriating the Pharisees and scribes. The important point is this: Jesus accepted people for who they were. Romans or Jews. Sinners like Simon Peter and ascetics like John the Baptist. Women of majestic virtue and ladies of the street. Does it seem a stretch that Jesus would also affirm the right of people to be whatever God created them to be in matters of sexual orientation? Not to me.

Dear Tom: I am a woman of color, and every day I hear others, who claim to be Christians, making ignorant remarks that show their obvious prejudices of other races. Is there a verse in the Bible that covers this issue? I would like to show them, in verses, where this is not God's intention for people to be so hateful. Please help me.
— **J.S., via Internet**

Dear J.S.: I'm really not a big fan of proof-texting, but try this one: "There is no longer Jew or Greek, there is no longer slave or free, there is no longer male and female; for all of you are one in Christ Jesus" (Galatians 3:28). In New Testament times, three-fourths of the people in Roman society were slaves (the word is often translated "servants"). Most of them were of disparate racial groups, blackest African to blondest Northern European. So the idea that Jew or Greek, slave or free, male or female are "one in Christ Jesus" pretty much covers universal equality for the human family.

Yes, other verses have been taken out of context to show superiority or inferiority of this or that group. When a 21st-century person uses a few obscure biblical passages to justify racial slurs, my advice is simple: Do not dignify those comments with a response. Jesus did not come to save this race or that, but to teach everyone who found his way appealing. The great religious teachers of humanity have been unanimous on this point. Mohammed certainly didn't care what color a believer was, nor did Buddha.

The only people who proclaim racism as a religious doctrine are ignorant and self-serving unfortunates who have tuned away from the Divine Truth about the oneness of humanity. They prowl the shadow side of religion, like a flock of dinosaurs looking for a tar pit. Stand aside and let them go. On the brighter side, God loves us all ... even the bigots. So sooner or later, we'll get it right.

Dear Tom: I heard a speaker mention the "seven undisputed letters of Paul" and wondered what she meant by that. Are there disputed letters? Who is doing the disputing?
— **C.C., Kansas City, Missouri**

Dear C.C.: She was mentioning the widely held idea that we possess seven letters actually written (probably dictated) by the apostle himself. "Undisputed" means that no serious scholar—conservative or liberal—doubts their authenticity as letters by Paul. The seven letters are 1 Thessalonians, 1 and 2 Corinthians, Philippians, Romans, Galatians and Philemon. In these works we can we feel reasonably safe that Paul is speaking directly to us across the centuries.

The answer to the other part of your question—are there disputed letters?—seems a natural consequence of this first point, that is, if we have seven which are not disputed, Pauline authorship of the others must be controversial. Scholars usually divide the pack of 13 letters (or 14 with Hebrews) attributed to Paul in four parts. The first, "undisputed letters," we have already discussed. Next are the "deutero-Pauline" epistles of 2 Thessalonians, Colossians and Ephesians. These are controversial, and the dispute sometimes breaks down along conservative-liberal lines (conservatives say *yes*, liberals say *no*). However, there are enough textual differences and theological quirks between these and the undisputed letters that most serious scholars are suspicious of their origins. Ephesians is often flatly dismissed as non-Pauline, although the jury is still out on the other two.

The third category is called the "Pastoral Letters" and consists of 1 and 2 Timothy and Titus. These are universally regarded as works of the Pauline school, meaning those who came after the apostle and wrote what they considered his kind of ideas, attributing the documents to Paul. These three "letters" were addressed to people in ministry and thus the term *pastoral* is often applied. Finally there is the Letter to the Hebrews, which earns its own category because it never even claims to be written by Paul. The language and content of this lengthy treatise make Pauline authorship of Hebrews highly dubious. Nevertheless, some conservative interpreters insist it was written by Paul anyway.

Now since the original documents are long gone and all we have are copies of copies of copies, there is no way to know for certain which views are correct. However, I tend to agree with the evaluation of progressive scholars. They say it is possible to tell the difference between Paul's genuine writing and pseudo-Pauline work, just as we could easily tell the difference between English authors Charles Dickens and J.K. Rowling. Even so, all these letters or epistles or whatever you call them can be vehicles for insight and inspiration, which is an undisputed fact affirmed by conservatives and liberals alike.

-14-

God in the Hebrew Bible

Dear Tom: I am writing in response to your answer in the May 1995 issue: I feel your answer was wrong and has misled people. You are giving people the wrong picture of God. Yes, God is loving, forgiving, merciful, healing and much more. God does want us to share eternity with Him, but not everyone will go to heaven. I don't see how you can say not to be frightened by eternal punishment. The Bible says there is eternal punishment: it's not a fantasy; it is eternal, everlasting. Perhaps you are one of those who are so engrossed in God's love, mercy and forgiveness that you are forgetting or ignoring that God is a judge and will punish. The Bible tells us so.

— **K.K., Williamsport, Pennsylvania**

Dear K.K.: Where do I begin? You have correctly identified a common belief in antiquity—that people are inherently evil and need punishment unless somehow transformed by a saving event. And, yes, the biblical Jesus speaks in these terms. But the uncomfortable truth about the Gospels is they were not written by Jesus, but the second and third generations of the Church. The Gospels are, at best, repositories for memories about what Jesus said. You will find no doctrine of eternal punishment in the only authentic first-generation writings we have, the seven letters of St. Paul. If you read a good, modern translation—like Today's English Version or the Revised Standard Version—you'll see Paul believes that the wicked will cease to exist. He often calls it "eternal destruction," a very Jewish position. Some Unity thinkers take this as metaphysical description of what happens when we turn completely away from God's goodness. We suffer as long as we turn away from God. When we turn back to God, wickedness ceases to exist.

The idea of eternal punishment is offensive to moral and ethical standards. If you were punishing someone who really deserved it—a serial killer, a genocidal maniac like Hitler—how long could you stand to hear him suffer? And if you know that everlasting torture is wrong, don't you think God knows too?

Finally, could you really worship a God who allows hell to exist, who allows anybody to suffer for all eternity? When reflecting on life after death in all its speculative possibilities, my rule is "Trust God, and let eternity take care of itself."

Dear Tom: Regarding your response to one of your letters, you state that God doesn't get angry. Come

on, Mr. Shepherd; get real. How can anyone who's cracked a Bible say, "God doesn't get angry"?
— **G.J., Cedar Ridge, California**

Dear G.J.: The God of Israel was anthropomorphic, and unavoidably so. The Bible was not lowered from heaven in a basket; it was written by men. Inspired men, certainly, but men, no less. (As far as we know, no women authors contributed manuscripts to the biblical library. No surprise, in patriarchal Israel.) Because the authors were men, they endowed their Creator with the basic features of human males. God extended His hand, inclined His ear, and turned His face away—all body parts belonging to human beings. A psalmist or two may have waxed poetic about being covered by God's feathers and taking shelter under His wings, but to my knowledge no theologian has ever argued that God is shaped like a big chicken. The God of Israel—Who could not be pictured in Hebrew art because that would have been idolatry—nevertheless was envisioned in the shape of a man. The author of Genesis defends this notion in reverse when God decides to make man in His image. If we look like God, God must look like us.

As well as making their God anthropomorphic, the biblical authors picture their God as anthropopathic—they give Him human emotions: He loves, hates, gets jealous and flares with anger. He also changes His mind, "repents" of the evil He has decided to do, and lets several biblical characters talk Him into another course of action.

The Bible is a human document containing Divine inspiration. It is our challenge to find, in the primitive understandings of men who lived thousands of years ago, the eternal message of God's love, power and presence. That's why the supreme model for God in the Western world isn't the anthropomorphic-anthropopathic god. God is revealed to us in Jesus the Christ. When we see Jesus, we see what God is like.

Now you could argue that Jesus drove the money changers out of the temple, and he showed anger on several other occasions. True. But when he finally achieved full God-consciousness at the end of his earthly life, his last words were unmitigated love and forgiveness, even for those who nailed him to the cross. That's a much better God model than an all-powerful being with a temper problem, don't you think?

Dear Tom: I am from Colombia (I speak Spanish) and I am learning to let go of all my fears, the "obstacles" that stop me from being the person God wants me to be. My two daughters will learn their ABCs at school, but will learn about God with me. Every time I open a Bible, it talks about God sending suffering because people were bad—God punishing us! This doesn't make sense to me. I wonder if you know of a book, especially a Bible, I can read to my girls that doesn't talk about a God who hurts us, because I know that is not true.

— **R.P., Portage, Mississippi**

Dear R.P.: Try *Jonathan Livingston Seagull* by Richard Bach. As for biblical books, read to them from the Gospels, the Letter of Paul to the Philippians, and the Acts of the Apostles. Most children love Psalms and Proverbs too. I'd get them a modern translation, like the New Revised Standard Version, if you'll be reading in English. But don't be limited to the words of others. Tell your children the Bible stories as you would repeat a good tale you heard at camp. It is no accident that much of our religious literature has come down to us as story, parable and poetry. People told the good news before anyone set pen to paper.

> Dear Tom: In the past few weeks I have heard three different television ministers state that the earth was created 10,000 years ago and that there is a period of 4,000 years from Adam to Jesus. Since these statements are absurd in view of all scientific knowledge, my question is, What are these people basing their claims on?
>
> — **D.F., Oklahoma City, Oklahoma**

Dear D.F.: Many televangelists are progressive thinkers, but not all. The preachers you describe subscribe to the so-called young-earth theory. In fact, some Christian groups say that the world was created quite recently. Young-earth theorists often call upon the fallacious logic of 17th-century Anglican Archbishop James Ussher. The British churchman added up all the Old Testament genealogies and decided Creation had taken place on October 23, 4004 B.C., at 9 a.m. (*No, really—I'm not making this up!*)

Without even considering that most geologists put the age of the earth at 4.5 billion years, the city of Jericho has existed since 8000 B.C., which means it must have been hanging in empty space 4,000 years by Ussher's timetable. Ussher's mistake was blessed by second- and-third-generation editors of the King James Bible, who included the Bishop's Creation chronology as if it were part of the Greek and Hebrew text. Modern fundamentalists probably picked up the idea from the later King James editions, without any knowledge of the archbishop's boo-boo. Over 100 editions of the King James Bible have been printed. Editors have frequently changed the text or added materials to suit their political, social and theological whims. Not surprisingly, the anti-evolutionist camp still loves Bishop Ussher's math.

Dear Tom: I would like to know about your biblical knowledge on the subject of eating pork. One television minister said hogs eat anything; therefore the meat is laced with bacteria. A Jewish friend said gentiles raise hogs, so the Jews are not to eat pork. My theory is pork was forbidden due to no refrigeration, so it was harmful, not sinful, to eat. Who is correct?

— **W.C., Castroville, California**

Dear W.C.: Everybody but the minister. The Hebrews saw themselves as an ark of ethically correct, God-fearing people, adrift in a sea of immoral, idol-worshiping heathens. Since the marriage feast of the Palestinian gentiles included ritual slaughter of swine and eating of shellfish, laws against those two foods effectively cut off marriage contracts between Jew and non-Jew. Secondly, pork does spoil quickly with disastrous results; Jews who refrained from porcine products stayed healthier throughout history. There is no evidence, to my knowledge, that pigs are any dirtier in their eating habits than goats and cattle, both of which are kosher (okay to eat). Pigs get a bum rap because they cool themselves with mud. Ask any pig farmer—hogs are smart, healthy and— unfortunately for them—a tasty source of lean protein when properly cooked.

Dear Tom: I am concerned about your answer about eating pork. We are told that meat, poultry and fish are poisons. Meat and poultry are polluted in our filthy processing plants. And fish are polluted in our polluted rivers, lakes and oceans. So we should all be vegetarians, as I am. With best wishes for your continuing loving service to our Master and us.

— R.W. (no city/state provided)

Dear R.W.: I didn't expect the flurry of letters after my brief comment about pork being wholesome fare. Yours was one of the nicer ones—thank you very much. One lady suggested I had probably killed a lot of people who might begin eating pork because of my answer. The anti-pork coalition seems to include 1) vegetarians like yourself, 2) animal rights folks who believe we should eat no flesh, 3) super-health-food people who insist that pork is bad food, and 4) kosher keepers, since pork is outlawed in the Torah. With all due respect to the faxes and letters I've received that detail the sins of the pig and the dangers of consuming its "bacteria and worms"—I stand by what I wrote.

Naturally, anyone who wants to avoid meat for religious or ethical reasons should not eat pork. However, an overwhelming weight of scientific evidence shows that pork is wholesome and healthy to eat when properly prepared. It is red meat and not, as the pork industry wants us to believe, "the other white meat."

Dr. John DeLecuona, staff physician at the Medical College of Georgia and a family friend, said the following: "Pigs are healthy animals. But like all animals, they have a risk of parasites." John says the key is to cook the meat thoroughly. My doctor friend also cautions against dietary extremism: "Vegetarian diets usually don't provide all the protein human bodies need, which is why most vegetarians supplement with milk, eggs or fish."

There are risks with animal proteins, but not the kind usually highlighted by nonscientific anti-meat literature. Dr. DeLecuona says moderation is the key: "Animal meat benefits must be balanced by keeping overall fat calories down."

It seems to me that common sense and clean living are far more important than trying to follow impossibly strict dietary rules. Catholic and Orthodox Christian monastics are known for their abstinence from meat during special holy periods, sometimes permanently. Seventh Day Adventists recommend vegetarianism, as do many Quakers and New Thought Christians.

Since I write this column for *Unity Magazine*, I would be remiss if I did not mention that the Unity movement was influenced on this subject by the vegetarianism of co-founder Charles Fillmore. However, Mr. Fillmore never made anti-meat a doctrine of faith, and today Unity people typically follow the eclectic dietary patterns of religious progressives everywhere. Moderation seems to be the key. I heard the late Ernest Wilson, who was a lifelong friend of the Fillmores and one of the first Unity ministers, say that Charles Fillmore— good vegetarian though he was—sometimes sneaked out for a hamburger. In all fairness to the vegetarians among us, when I asked Mr. Fillmore's granddaughter, Rosemary Fillmore Rhea, about Ernest Wilson's report she expressed doubts about the story. So there are mixed opinions on how rigorous the Unity movement has been in vegetarianism. It was never a requirement for ministry or membership.

Dear Tom: I would appreciate any help you can give me in understanding the Bible and using it effectively to enrich my spiritual life. When I tried reading the entire Bible a couple of years ago, I found it impossible to wade through the genealogies and "rules and regulations" about how the temple was

to be built, and so forth. Is there any reason to read through all that detail today, or is it only relevant in historical context?
— **A.I., Hillsboro, Oregon**

Dear A.I.: The Bible isn't a book; it's a library. Actually, it's more like an anthology—fully of stories, sacred histories, law codes, legends, myths, poetry, praise, prayers, personal and community letters, essays and lots more.

Get yourself a good historical commentary, like the *Interpreter's One-Volume Commentary on the Bible*, and study with it open on your desk.

Dear Tom: What is meant by the reference to a "whisperer" in Proverbs 18:8?
— **H.S., Amarillo, Texas**

Dear H.S.: The Revised Standard Version (RSV) translates Proverbs 18:8 as follows: *"The words of a whisperer are like delicious morsels; they go down into the inner parts of the body."* Since I don't read Hebrew, I checked several biblical commentaries, but they left me in the dark. Then I looked in two other Bible translations, and the lights came on. The Jerusalem Bible renders the passage this way: *"The words of a talebearer are tasty morsels."* But the most helpful translation was Today's English Version (TEV): *"Gossip is so tasty—how we love to swallow it!"* Does that help?

Dear Tom: I've always wondered about Psalm 22:6 (KJV), which reads, "But I am a worm, and no man; a reproach of men, and despised of the people." As I understand it, this verse refers to Christ as being the Son of God. How is it that he can say that he is a worm? Your comments on this will be greatly appreciated.

— **E.K., Yoakum, Texas**

Dear E.K.: Thanks for your expression of confidence. The New Revised Standard Version renders this passage slightly differently, "scorned by others, and despised by the people," which makes a little more sense to modern readers. It is not likely the Hebrew author, writing centuries before the Christian Era, was thinking about Jesus Christ when he penned this psalm.

Taken as a whole, Psalm 22 charts in wavelike pattern the rise and fall of the psalmist's mood as he contemplated life. It begins with the most terrifying sentence in the Bible, uttered again by Jesus Christ on the cross: "My God, my God, why hast thou forsaken me?" and ends with an appeal for "the coming generation" of young Israelites to "proclaim his deliverance to a people yet unborn."

Jesus probably said those words in praying the psalm aloud. It was the custom in the ancient world to blare the first and last lines of a prayer. The last words of this psalm, "he has wrought it," could be stretched to mean "it is finished," which was another of the reported last sayings of Jesus at Calvary.

What about the meaning of this psalm for today? Well, I'm with you. I don't like to think of myself as a worm, not even on a bad day. But I understand how someone could feel that low, don't you? After all, some churches have told people for centuries that they are lowly sinners; a worm isn't much of a step down from that. I try to hold to Truth principles when these feelings of woeful inadequacy arise. I know that each sentient being is a child of God, filled with wisdom, peace and light. The problem isn't inadequacy, it's disbelief. If I truly believe in the Christ within, if I take seriously the divine Presence and Power, no circumstance can plunge me willy-nilly into lamentations. Despair cannot continue to plague me when I realize that God is the One Presence/One Power working in and through all things. For me, that's the real message of Psalm 22, and Calvary's cross as well.

Dear Tom: After God made Adam and Eve, they had Cain and Abel. Then Cain married a woman and had Enoch. Who was this woman that Cain married (Genesis 4)? Was she from Nod, east of Eden? Was she a descendant of Adam and Eve?
— R.X., via Internet

Dear R.X.: Sometimes, when I'm asked, "Where did Cain get his wife" I'm tempted to reply, "Haven't you seen *Fiddler on the Roof?* Like any traditional Jewish kid—the families arranged the wedding!" All these characters are legendary, not historical figures. Sometimes, stories are just stories.

Asking where Cain got his wife is like asking Donald Duck to prove he isn't the biological father of Huey, Dewey and Louie. Good stories tell us about real life, sometimes better than verbatim transcripts. Jesus told stories. So did all the great teachers of humanity. It's the meaning of the stories, not their historical accuracy, that makes them worthwhile.

Dear Tom: What are your thoughts on this verse: "And as it is appointed unto men once to die, but after this the judgment" (Hebrews 9:27)? I get hammered with this when trying to explain that hell is in the mind, not an eternal pit of foul smoke, deadly gases and rotten blood. Also, how does this die-once idea apply to reincarnation?
— **M.A.S., Escondido, California**

Dear M.A.S.: The text you quoted is often taken as a one-liner, out of context with the passage in which it is embedded. The Letter to the Hebrews was written by an unknown first-century Christian, not Paul. If you read Hebrews 9:23-27—or better yet, the whole ninth chapter of the book—you'll see verse 27 was a marker phrase, thrown off by the author to establish a logical comparison between the mythology of human existence after death and the mythological experiences he is narrating about the risen Lord's duties in heaven for the sake of humanity.

> For Christ did not enter a sanctuary made by human hands, a mere copy of the true one, but he entered into heaven itself, now to appear in the presence of God on our behalf (Hebrews 9:24).

The author of Hebrews ties down the imagery with a much-quoted aside about humanity:

> And just as it is appointed for mortals to die once, and after that the judgment, so Christ, having been offered once to bear the sins of many, will appear a second time, not to deal with sin, but to save those who are eagerly waiting for him (Hebrews 9:27-28).

It is clear the focus of his argument has nothing to do with whether humans live and die but once—which would, of course, rule out reincarnation—but rather speaks to the sacrificial offering of the blood of Jesus to cleanse humanity of its sins. Taken at face value, blood atonement is a bizarre, odious idea to the modern mind. But this passage, in fact the entire Bible, was not written for the modern mind. Animal sacrifice was a widespread practice in the ancient world. The idea was that the offenses which humans committed frequently offended the divine power(s), which could be placated by offering the appropriate recompense. Doves for little offenses; bulls for the big sins. Of course, the priests who offered sacrifices usually got to keep a portion of the meat in payment.

Animal sacrifice to re-establish balance between heaven and earth was so prevalent that almost all animals killed in Greek and Roman cities were offered to some god or another.

Why waste the life of the animal when you could get it butchered and get your sins forgiven in one-stop shopping? This caused problems for the Christian community, because the back doors of the pagan temples were literally the city meat markets. How could Christians eat meat, since it was all the product of a pagan ritual?

Paul answers this question at length in his First Letter to the Corinthians (Chapters 8-11). Here's an excerpt:

> Now concerning food sacrificed to idols: ... "Food will not bring us close to God." We are no worse off if we do not eat, and no better off if we do. But take care that this liberty of yours does not some-how become a stumbling block to the weak (1 Corinthians 8:1, 8-9).

Paul is essentially saying: "Well ... yeah, dude. Eat what you want. God doesn't care, because the idols are stone images, not rival gods. Unless it's a problem for you—or it causes simpler members of the community to be confused—go for it." Paul shows his pragmatic side here. He has one agenda only: to get the new message of Christ consciousness out to as many people as possible.

As far as hell is concerned, you won't find it in the undisputed Letters of Paul because he didn't believe in it. Paul is an extinctionist, one who believes the unbelievers are headed for nonbeing. He called it *destruction*. "For them this is evidence of their destruction, but of your salvation" (Philippians 1:28).

Regardless of their eternal destinies, lost and saved souls are problematic to 21st-century people, and the concept of placating the Divine wrath through the slaughter of lambs or doves is morally reprehensible. How much more repugnant would it be to sacrifice a human? What kind of deity would demand this, and what kind of religionist would worship a god like that? Does God really require the death of Jesus to soothe His anger-management problem? If so, shame on Him. And shame on us for promoting such a monstrous absurdity for 2,000 years. God is love, and love wants nothing but love in return.

Dear Tom: I need a more spiritual answer to one of the commandments the Lord gave us, "Thou shall not kill." My clear feeling on this is that the Lord meant not to kill any human or animal. Killing for survival may be okay, but otherwise—that is, to enjoy, consume, eat—it is against the Lord's Word and should be against the conscience of any person. Can you please expand on this for me?
— **L.H., London, U.K.**

Dear L.H.: This is a highly controversial subject, and I want to answer you authentically. But I need to say, up front, that my reply is *not* the official word on the topic, just one theologian's point of view. So please feel free to disagree.

I can understand the desire to find biblical warrant for pacifism and ethical vegetarianism. However, the Hebrew Scripture doesn't broadly support those commendable ambitions. You quoted the sixth commandment (Exodus 20:13), which is usually rendered differently in modern translations, like the New Revised Standard Version: "You shall not murder."

Some scholars have observed that the Ten Commandments were traditionally given to Moses on Mount Sinai before the conquest of Canaan land by the children of Israel. An armed horde about to cross the river and attack every city in their path was hardly poised at the brink of a Gandhi-esque outbreak of pacifism. Most historians believe the book of Exodus was not a firsthand account by Moses but a carefully assembled consolidation of centuries of ideas, written down after the Israelites had already become the dominant people in their "Promised Land."

A commandment against killing in warfare makes no sense in the history of Israel. The Israelites repeatedly defended their claim to the biblical lands by armed force, often to their utter destruction in battle, at least in ancient times. Yet Hebrew prophets never seemed to question the *ethics* of warfare, just the wisdom of waging it during any given period. More recently, most Jewish scholars—who know their Scripture quite intimately—have interpreted the sixth commandment as permitting self-defense to fend off Israel's increasingly hostile regional neighbors.

Although fighting in warfare is permissible in Hebrew thought, some Christian scholars contend that armed conflict becomes more difficult to justify when confronted by the Jesus Christ ethos of "love thy enemy." While lacking space in a brief answer to develop this line of argument fully, let's just say some commentators have noted that Jesus never called for disbandment of defensive forces or police, nor did he condemn the military personnel with whom he interacted. In fact, Luke 7 reports Jesus praising one Roman centurion's faith as greater than anything he had experienced in the House of Israel. And all four Gospels agree that the Prince of Peace himself drove corrupt money changers from the outer grounds of the Jerusalem temple. Needless to say, there is a lively debate about whether Jesus was a true pacifist, and I invite you to read the arguments on both sides.

To interpret the commandment as a call to vegetarianism is even more problematic, considering Israelites took leave of Egypt for the express purpose of offering animal sacrifice in the wilderness. The formula is repeated several times throughout the Exodus story: Say to him (Pharaoh), the Lord, the God of the Hebrews, sent me to you to say, "Let my people go, so that they may worship me in the wilderness."[1]

By definition, *to worship* meant offering animal sacrifice. Nothing else was considered *worship* in the ancient world. Prayer, songs, meditation and other rites were supportive of the central act which made the event a "worship" experience; that is, the ritual slaughter of a living animal. And this included not just the Jews but the whole Hellenistic (Greco-Roman) world. The back doors of pagan temples were often the town butcher shops, where people bought their meats after the animal had been properly cut and prepared. This is the cultural dilemma faced by Paul, who basically told the church at Corinth: If eating meat offered to idols bothers you or confuses others, don't do it. Otherwise, not a problem (1 Corinthians 8).

But there are other voices in Scripture too. In time of war, such as we are now experiencing, people often find the

Hebraic vision of beating swords into plowshares and the New Testament call for reconciliation in Christ to be supportive images for the long-term peace of this planet. Although I respect the ardent pacifists and vegetarians among us, my understanding of Christian ethics allows me to consume animal products and support a just war. There are many important things to be said on both sides of these issues, and I've decided to keep an open mind and let wiser minds discuss this at length. But for now at least, a juicy hamburger and a strong national defense still sound like good ideas to me.

Dear Tom: My question regards abortion, when life begins, and if God esteems the life of a fetus/unborn child as highly as that of a living child. Several years ago a letter to the editor in my hometown newspaper brought up a point that in one of the Old Testament books, probably Exodus but maybe Deuteronomy, there was a case on point that was the only reference to the issue in the Bible. A person wrongfully injured or killed a pregnant woman and her living child. As punishment to the wrongful party, the Lord authorized a payment of two heads of cattle (goats, maybe) for each living person whose life was lost, but only one head of cattle for the unborn child. To take the point a step further in context of the biblical judgment, it seems to be saying that what is in the best interest of a pregnant woman is twice as important as her unborn child. Do you agree?

— S.K., Terre Haute, Indiana

Dear S.K: You are referring to Exodus 21:22. Actually, the text in the New Revised Standard Version is even more compelling in its argument for two tiers of liability:

> When people who are fighting injure a pregnant woman so that there is a miscarriage, and yet no further harm follows, the one responsible shall be fined what the woman's husband demands, paying as much as the judges determine.[2]

However, the real question isn't "What did tribal judges believe 3,000 years ago in a society where women and children were little more than property?" The question is "What should we do today in the 21st century, where women and children have full human rights?"

I am frankly ambivalent and conflicted on this one. My head tells me the woman should have a right to control her body and choose whether to carry a fetus to term. My heart says, the *fetus* is a human being—what else could it be?—who is totally dependent upon its mother for existence itself. The arguments get more convoluted and emotional the more they are studied.

I know my readers are accustomed to snappy responses that my ego sometimes fires off too glibly, as though I could deal adequately with any question. But I don't have an answer for you on this question. I just trust God and the goodness of humanity to work it out. And it's going to take some time, because the jury of faith and the judgment of history are still out on this one. Whichever position you take, remember there are good people on the other side.

Good Questions

-15-

Reprogramming the Zeitgeist

Dear Tom: It seems that metaphysical Christianity is just a religion for middle- and upper-class Americans and that it emphasizes self-centeredness. For example, Charles Fillmore states, "If we would have peace and harmony in our environment, we must establish it within ourselves." How does this apply to the people in Darfur? No amount of "peace and harmony" within the inhabitants is going to stop the horrific genocide going on there. How do prosperity teachings apply to the people who live in Bangladesh or Somalia? Why doesn't metaphysical Christianity have missions established in the United States and the rest of the world to help alleviate poverty, disease and other problems? Why isn't there more outreach to follow in the footsteps of Jesus? I understand that prayer is extremely important, but as it says in the Epistle of James 2:14-17, faith without action is dead. These

things have bothered me for a long time, and I really need to hear from you.
— **C.B., Indianapolis, Indiana**

Dear C.B.: You've raised an important issue. Do the spiritual principles of metaphysical Christianity have anything to say about crushing poverty, true oppression, abusive circumstances, human cruelty, violence and other circumstances which are beyond the daily experience of middle-class congregations in the U.S. and Canada? (You must have known my answer would be "Yes," because anything else would probably require me to return my ordination certificate.)

Yes, prosperity principles will work in places where human needs are great. I've often heard it said that we are spiritual beings having a human experience. If this is true, then it is entirely possible for humans in dire circumstances to align themselves with the central Truth of the Universe—God is One Presence/One Power—and release the unlimited power of God in their lives. Metaphysical Christianity has discovered that one way to do this is by centering in the God-within-us by affirmative prayer. But even highly centered, deeply spiritual persons must admit that outside events have an effect on what happens to them. This is summarized in one of my favorite maxims: "There are no tiger gods where there are no tigers."

Take an example from U.S. history. Why did the vast majority of white people in the antebellum South support the institution of slavery, even though less than 25 percent of the population owned slaves? Was it just a coincidence, or did God just allow all the "bad" people to be born in the South?

Of course not. The Old South did not invent slavery; it was old as the Old Testament. Antebellum Dixie had merely adapted what it called the "peculiar institution" of slavery to its agrarian economy. Today we realize that *any* economy based on slave labor is an inhumane system, but white Southerners were born into that kind of social structure and accepted its values as normative.

And the Old South was not the only example of socially acceptable inhumanity. Aztec priests sacrificed thousands of slave-captives to their bloodthirsty gods; Germans allowed Hitler to plunge Europe into the Holocaust; African tribal warfare, today waged with automatic weapons, has been rightly called genocide ... How does this happen? How can so many people be so terribly off track?

You quoted Charles Fillmore in your question, so let me reply with another quote from my favorite modern mystic:

> The human race has formed laws of physical birth and death, laws of sickness and physical inability, laws making food the source of bodily existence, laws of mind that recognize no other source of existence except the physical.[1]

Fillmore's concept of "race consciousness," which has nothing to do with skin color or ethnicity, refers to the human race in general. Although Mr. Fillmore presents the concept to describe the harmful effects of human race consciousness, I like to think of it more broadly as the *zeitgeist*, the general attitude or mood of an age. There seems to be a group consciousness which pervades all cultures, and it can uplift people or hammer them down. We have seen the religious insanity of suicide bombers who have convinced themselves that God loves violence to accomplish divine goals. I would argue that the business of Christian communities throughout the ages has been to reprogram the current *zeitgeist* to reflect love of God and neighbor. Not everybody has understood this must include tolerance and diversity.

Your letter quoted from *Atom-Smashing Power of Mind.* Here is a more complete version of the quote:

> It is the law of Spirit that we must be that which we would draw to us. If we would draw to us love, we must be love, be loving and kind; if we would have peace and harmony in our environment, we must establish it within ourselves. We must faithfully and persistently deny the appearance of that which seems to be inharmonious and silently and faithfully affirm the omnipresent peace, love and harmony that we want to see manifested.[2]

Can you imagine what kind of a world we would have if people began programming peaceful thoughts into the human race consciousness, especially in troubled spots like Darfur? What could a positive change in the human race consciousness do if it were growing stronger in places of dire economic needs? Did Jesus feed the multitudes miraculously with the loaves and the fishes, or did he help people to raise their consciousness high enough to share the food they had been hoarding?

Missions is a word which has fallen on hard times, but I totally agree with your underlying suggestion, that positive-minded organizations should get intentional about going international. Not to convert the heathen, but to join with spiritually minded people everywhere to transform the world into a place where positive thoughts are part of the *zeitgeist* of the planet.

Dear Tom: I keep reading the newspaper and watching TV news and nothing is getting better. Do you think it's possible the Second Coming of Jesus is near, like in those *Left Behind* novels?
— **J.N., Atlanta, Georgia**

Dear J.N.: No, I don't think the world will end in a cataclysm heralded by angelic trumpets and showering stars. Every generation has some people who believe the world will end in their lifetimes, and this has been true from the first century to the 21st. I'm confident that in the year 3000 C.E., someone will ask the same question. We have problems as a human species, but we have magnificent potential too.

Look at the parable of the Prodigal Son in Luke 15:11-32. This young man made all the wrong choices. He ended up living far from home, penniless, slopping the hogs, with nothing to eat. Pretty bad space for a Jewish kid—begging for leftovers from the unkosher swine. And his misery was self-inflicted, as it usually is. He had spent his father's money on—these are the words of the text—prostitutes and wild living. At this point in the story, Jesus pays the human race an enormous compliment:

> But when he came to himself he said, "How many of my father's hired hands have bread enough and to spare, but here I am dying of hunger! I will get up and go to my father ...."[3]

The beautiful line in this text is "when he came to himself ...." With those words, Jesus was affirming that we have an internal balance mechanism; we have within us a good, sensible, loving self. The default position for humanity is not grubbing in a pigpen, it's at home with the Father. And in this story, the father doesn't come to him with trumpets and servants to rescue the kid from the muck. He has to get up, clean up and walk home.

So may I suggest that no matter how desperate the world situation may seem, we have a while. The rent is paid on this world until a few billion years from now, when the sun will swell into a red giant and scorch our lovely planet to stardust once more. Until then, let's get up, clean up, and head home—come to ourselves as a species, quit wasting time with the swine-thoughts of life, and recognize we're all part of the family of God.

Dear Tom: I've grown sick of our elected officials and their need to dig up dirt about political opponents. Does the Bible have any words of wisdom for times like these?
— E.Q., St. Louis, Missouri

Dear E.Q.: "Let anyone among you who is without sin be the first to throw a stone" (John 8:7) comes to mind. And the wisdom tradition in the Bible is pretty clear on this point: "Do not say, 'I will do to others as they have done to me; I will pay them back for what they have done'" (Proverbs 24:29).

If you've read early church history, you know there's nothing new about scandal-mongering. Roman political leaders blamed the Christian minority when fire swept the capital. The church leader Tertullian complained that no matter what happened—whether the Tiber rose or the Nile didn't—Christians got blamed. Metaphysical Christianity locates the problem and its solution by looking within, not by castigating others. Discovering sin within a neighbor's heart doesn't make me a better person. Leaders who instigate witch hunts simply advertise their devotion to fear. It is Jesus who takes the wisdom teaching one step further with an initiative for love: "In everything do to others as you would have them do to you; for this is the law and the prophets" (Matthew 7:12).

> Dear Tom: Is it true that President Kennedy used a Unity prayer during the Cuban Missile Crisis?
> — **D.M., Oakland, California**

Dear D.M.: Yes. The following information comes from my conversations with the late Rev. Bob Wasner, who was my good friend and fellow Unity minister. During the Cuban missile crisis, October 1962, Silent Unity quickly printed up and rush-mailed the following "Prayer for World Leaders" to its many correspondents: "Through the Christ-mind you are unified in thought, purpose and understanding for the security and freedom of all mankind." Apparently John F. Kennedy's secretary, Evelyn Lincoln, was on the Silent Unity mail list. When she got this prayer, she immediately gave it to the president, who put in on his desk. Time passed, the crisis thankfully abated, but the following autumn President Kennedy was murdered.

A week after the assassination, as Jacqueline Kennedy was clearing out his desk, she discovered the "Prayer for World Leaders." When she asked Ms. Lincoln about the prayer, the first lady learned about her husband's Silent Unity connection. Bob said Jackie promptly called Unity Village and spoke to May Rowland, who was then director of Silent Unity. Mrs. Kennedy told Ms. Rowland how much this prayer had meant to the president, especially during the dark, foreboding days of the Cuban Missile Crisis, when the world faced the very real possibility of nuclear annihilation. Rev. Wasner also reported that, during the missile crisis, Unity Village was designated a fallout shelter because of the tunnels and underground classroom spaces.

One further note: Rev. Bob was working the Silent Unity room when President Kennedy was assassinated. He says calls actually dropped off, and those that came in were mostly about the country. People had forgotten their personal problems and began praying for their nation and the grieving first family. It is amazing the good that prayer can do—then and now!

> Dear Tom: One of my greatest pleasures in life is to
> wander alone with God near a stream or through a
> park or woods. With the crime rate being what it is
> today, my family feels it is unsafe. Should I affirm
> the protection of God and continue anyway?
> — **S.G., Frederick, Maryland**

Dear S.G.: There is an Arabian proverb which goes, "Trust in
Allah, but tie your camel." You live in Maryland, a state
blessed with crowded cities and lonely forests. If you can get
away from town, a walk alone might not be unsafe. If you
must walk in metro areas, by all means affirm God's protection—but walk with a friend—during the daytime. God pro-
tects us, but God doesn't guarantee our safety if we're foolish.

> Dear Tom: It seems that there are new and even
> more terrible things happening these days—and
> that the world is out of control in some senses: car-
> jackings, school shootings, drive-by shootings, kids
> killing their parents and so forth. Kids seem to have
> lost their way. What is the cause, and what are some
> answers? Why is this happening?
> — **M.M., Augusta, Georgia**

Dear M.M.: I could suggest sociopsychological factors that
promote violence, but that's not why you wrote to an inspirational magazine. Those of us who follow the metaphysical

Christian path believe that all sentient beings have the Divine Presence within them. This includes not just exalted spiritual masters like Mohammed, Meister Eckhart, Moses Maimonides, Mahatma Gandhi and Mother Teresa, but also utter failures at enlightenment—the criminals, villains, thugs and brutes of every nation, creed and color.

This indwelling divine shard is often hard to see. How can we believe that Albert Schweitzer had no more divinity within him than Adolf Hitler since the two German-speakers represented the polar opposites of world-embracing selflessness and genocidal egotism? Yet every child in the cradle is a potential Schweitzer, Gandhi or Yogananda. Hitler could have avoided his heinous career if he had been willing to open his mind to the oneness of God, the oneness of humanity, and the oneness of Truth. But, like the drive-by shooters in the cities and the teenage terrorists from suburbia who kill their classmates with designer guns, every soul has to choose to affirm the good and deny the un-good (evil).

The choice to affirm life and love and oneness is always open to us. Unfortunately, not everyone makes the right choice at this stage of human spiritual evolution.

Dear Tom: Brother, I wanted to ask from your studies in Truth, what does Unity teach about warfare and violence for the Christian? Specifically, I was reading Leo Tolstoy's *The Kingdom of God Is Within You*, works of Gandhi and Dr. King, and I wondered if you believe that it is acceptable for a Christian to

take up arms for any government, or would they be more like the Quakers and believe in pacifism?
— **Rev. I.M., via Internet**

Dear I.M.: I suggest that pacifism is an *option*, not a requirement, for a follower of Jesus Christ. As I've said in different forums since September 11, the images we've seen of men and women going to extraordinary lengths to help their fellow humans in time of extreme peril—firefighters and police charging into collapsing buildings, ordinary citizens saving each other's lives, people working round-the-clock for months to dig through the wreckage in New York City—have evoked for me the biblical model of the Good Samaritan, who gave not because he would get anything in return but because it was the right thing to do. The Christ in me salutes the Christ in thee, and that is sufficient.

However, I've been rethinking some elements of the Good Samaritan parable, post-September 11. This is also a possible Unity view: When God calls somebody to be a Good Samaritan for people who are hurting, the Christ-centered person responds with generosity and love. *But then there are the robbers.* God may call somebody else to go back to the road junction and take care of the robbers, and that might involve the use of force for the good of all. Even though the Christ dwells within the robbers, one could argue that a morally responsible person would not allow the robbers to continue misusing their divine-human powers to harm other people. When it comes to specific details, the four Gospels agree on very little; however, Matthew, Mark, Luke and John unanimously report that Jesus drove the money changers out of the

Temple. Sometimes, you just have to do what is necessary to take care of the robbers.

There are limitations to this, of course. Even in a so-called just war (that is, war waged for the goals of justice, not conquest), violence is not a resolution of human problems. It's a surgical process at best, cutting into the body of humanity to drain the wounds of hatred and malice. In World War II, Allied nations fought to end Nazi terror and Japanese imperialism. But after the smoke of the battle had cleared, the world was a mess. It took constructive acts and generosity of spirit to rebuild cities devastated by war. And the world is still not the loving community that it could become, if the children of humanity embraced peace and equality for all.

Pacifism vs. "just war" is a personal choice. There is no "official" Christian position on the subject, because this is a moral decision which must be made from where you are, based on your insights into the nature of life and the promptings of the Christ-spirit within you.

Dear Tom: How would you respond to someone who is picketing the funerals of soldiers killed in Iraq on the premise that the USA is being punished by God because our nation is too permissive with homosexuality? (Not that it matters, but the dead soldiers themselves were not gay.) And the organization doing the picketing claims to be a Christian church!

— L.W, Spokane, Washington

Dear L.W: If I answer your question just as written—"How would you respond to ...?" My honest reply would have to be, "Rather badly, I think." Although the extremist group to which you are referring claims to be a Christian church, I am reminded of what Corrie Ten Boom's father told her in *The Hiding Place*: "A mouse might be in a cookie jar but he is not a cookie ..."

I visited the Web site of the "Christian" organization which is doing the picketing, and although I have seen a fair amount of breathtaking ignorance in my 60-plus years on the planet, this movement has reached a level of imperious rancor which goes beyond WWII Nazi propaganda. Much of its rhetoric is frankly too inflammatory to reproduce on this page, but the gist of it is that the USA has turned aside from God by promoting homosexuality; therefore, God is punishing us by sending our sons and daughters home in body bags. The Web site proudly proclaims "Thank God for IEDs" (Improvised Explosive Devices). Members of this "church" picket funerals of Americans killed in combat, holding up signs like "Thank God for maimed soldiers." They also say the idea that God loves everyone is "the greatest lie ever told" and demand that all nations impose the death penalty upon homosexuals. I am glad I'm no longer a military chaplain, because if I were conducting a funeral for a soldier killed in combat and someone appeared waving the kind of signs mentioned above—I'm ordinarily a nice guy, but I think I'd lose it.

Although it masquerades as a church, nothing can turn this rodent organization into a Christian cookie. The Gospel of Jesus Christ brings us a vision of a Father-Mother God who loves all people with wild abandon. And let's remember one irrefutable fact of history: Jesus was crucified because of religious zealots, not because decadent Rome spurned his God. This is not the first time hate mongers have tried to invoke Christian imagery—after all, the swastika is a hooked cross, and the KKK uses a burning cross as its primary symbol.

Okay, I need to pause and get centered. You can tell this topic pushes some of my buttons. I wanted to reproduce these ideas only to encourage you to be aware of the problem, not to give any power to the negatives. Frankly this torrent of anti-Christian and anti-American illogic is unworthy of refutation. And I encourage all my readers to pray for the healing wisdom and peace of Christ to surround everyone in these circumstances—especially the families of soldiers who have paid the ultimate price in their country's service. We are all one in God, and everyone has the Christ Spirit within them. As the apostle Paul said in one of his best moments of clarity, "There is no longer Jew or Greek, there is no longer slave or free, there is no longer male and female; for all of you are one in Christ Jesus" (Galatians 3:28).

I have one more point to offer in this discussion: Would it not be better for people to turn from condemning the lifestyle or values of others and invest their energies in praying for world peace? Here is a prayer I wrote a few years ago to encourage everyone to meditate on world peace. Prayer, of course, works anytime, but I was thinking how grand it would be if people around the world prayed for peace every day at noon, wherever they were. Think of the prayer rolling across the globe, never ceasing, as people lift their hearts to God and envision the world as it could be. It is a captivating vision. And so, I invite everyone to join the Noonday Peace Prayer movement!

Noonday Prayer for World Peace
By Thomas Shepherd

In unity with all my brothers and sisters of the human family, I call upon the presence and power of God to inspire the warring peoples of humanity to release all thoughts of hostility and transform this world into a garden of prosperity and peace. World peace is established now. Thank You, God.

Dear Tom: Is there any message of hope for the world when we continue to make war on one another with such passion? As I read the news, I get depressed.
— M.G., Chicago, Illinois

Dear M.G.: I submit to you the Christmas story: God-with-us, breaking into time and space through the presence of a baby in a manger. Even in the worst of times—which I am not going to affirm that we are experiencing—we know we are not alone. We shall not, like an ordinary day in the life of Ebenezer Scrooge, have to go to our cold, dark mansions and dine in terrible isolation. We are members of a community; we are part of the family of humanity; we are children of the cosmos, brothers and sisters of the stars, linked together by this mystical, delicious, empowering thing called *conscious-ness*.

That is why we need Christmas. We need to know the Christ—Divine Heart, throbbing at the center of the Universe; Divine Mind, creating and expanding the potential for good-ness—we need to know the Christ *has* come, is come, and evermore *will* come into the ordinary moments, the manger-moments of our lives. We need to keep our thoughts centered in the Christ, despite any appearances to the contrary.

To use a biblical metaphor, God does not promise to deliver us from the Romans; God promises to deliver the Romans to us. That's what happens when we learn to truly love our enemies. Eventually, enemies become our people and we become their people, because we're all one in the Spirit, united by our common indwelling divine nature.

God does not promise to remove all suffering and trouble at the first opportunity. God promises to turn suffering and trouble *into* opportunities, regardless of appearances to the contrary. And here's the exciting part ... better health, increased prosperity, improved relationships, greater self-esteem and a deeper spiritual life are all the by-products of learning to turn to the God within you. These are Christmas gifts which never stop giving. And what better time to affirm peace on earth than the season when we celebrate the birth of the Prince of Peace?

Dear Tom: Is there a good prayer I could send family members overseas in the military? I wish everyone could have a happy, prosperous, and

joyful holiday season this year, but I worry for their safety.
— **A.W., Fort Worth, Texas**

Dear A.W.: The "Prayer for Protection" by James Dillet Freeman, which was written for soldiers during the tumultuous days of World War II, comes immediately to mind:

> The light of God surrounds me;
> The love of God enfolds me;
> The power of God protects me;
> The presence of God watches over me.
> Wherever I am, God is!

Sometimes we need prayer more than other times. Joy may not always accompany us, because life does bring challenges. We see your loved ones surrounded by God's light, love and protection in any circumstance.

-16-

Life, Death, Eternity

Dear Tom: I have a friend who fears death and is confused as to what happens at the time of death. I am also confused. Please, help us out.
— **K.A., New Orleans, Louisiana**

Dear K.A.: Nobody knows for certain what happens at the moment of death, but the classic book in this field, Raymond A. Moody Jr.'s *Life After Life*, provides some hints. Dr. Moody studied hundreds of subjects who experienced clinical death, that is, whose hearts stopped beating so that they were momentarily considered dead by others. Moody discovered key similarities in these experiences no matter what religion the person practiced.

Often, the "deceased" person travels down a long tunnel to be greeted by the spirits of friends and relatives who have already died, and a beam of light appears before the person. The person approaches a barrier, but instead of crossing over, he is returned to the body. When people try to explain this experience to others, they find words to be inadequate. They never fear death again.[1]

Although beyond this we do not know the details of an afterlife, many great prophets and teachers—including Jesus and Mohammed—affirmed that such a life exists. It is in touching the presence of God in the stillness of prayer that we have the assurance of life eternal.

Dear Tom: I've always wondered if our loved ones who have died know what is happening down here. Can they come and be here and we not be able to see them? There are times I wish they knew what we have done, like the books I have written, but of course, if they could see the good, they could also know the bad things. I sometimes find stories that sound very convincing, stories of the Spirit leaving the body, then re-entering it. Can you help me?
— **L.M., Woodstock, Vermont**

Dear L.M.: Fascinating question, and a toughie. People have told me about near-death experiences in which they have seen their bodies from the outside, met with departed loved ones, and returned to describe what happened. Of course, skeptics say these people weren't really brain-dead; they merely dreamed these events as living beings, not as departed souls.

I'd like to think people who have gone beyond this world have the option to visit their loved ones here, but that remains in the realm of pure speculation. We simply don't know.

My grandmother, who raised me, made her transition in 1989. About a year before she died, I said, "Mom, if you get to heaven before I do, find out what I'm getting wrong in my theology and let me know somehow." She nodded in a very Pennsylvania Dutch way and said okay. I was joking, but she took the commission seriously. Many times I've felt her love surrounding me. Even though I've never had anything remotely resembling a psychic experience—nor would I seek one—I'd love for Grandmom Quell to know the good things that have happened in my life: growth and joy of my children, continuing happiness I've found in my marriage to Carol-Jean, and so many good experiences in the writing and teaching ministry. I miss her, but I can wait. No doubt Grandmom Quell has her work, too, and someday she'll tell me what I've missed in the grand scheme of things.

Dear Tom: Often we think of "eternal life" as something that is to come, when the word eternal implies it's here now, always has been, and always will be. Mind-boggling concept! Could that be the case?
— **M.R., Berkeley Springs, West Virginia**

Dear M.R.: I completely agree. Eternity has neither beginning nor ending. Look at the Christmas season. When reading the birth narratives of Jesus, most people look to Matthew and Luke—manger, star, Wise Men, shepherds (my favorites). But

The Gospel According to John offers another glimpse into where Jesus came from.

> In the beginning was the Word, and the Word was with God, and the Word was God. He was in the beginning with God. All things came into being through him, and without him not one thing came into being. What has come into being in him was life, and the life was the light of all people.[2]

Now some might say that refers exclusively to Jesus Christ, but metaphysical Christians believe that everything spiritual which can be claimed about Jesus can also be identified in each person. Jesus was what we shall become—or, what we ought to be already.

That means all of us existed "before the world was created," and Divinity expresses Itself through us. We are all incarnations of the divine word, born in the mangers of this world to learn about our oneness with the Father. And we have *forever* to get it right. What a terrific Christmas present!

Dear Tom: I would deeply appreciate the guidance and peace of mind you can bring to me concerning the hereafter and once again being with those I love so very much. I noted, too, you are a retired Army chaplain. Like so many, my husband served his country in World War II, lost his life returning from

a bombing mission at age 28 and was never found
in the North Sea.

— **C.B., Reno, Nevada**

Dear C.B.: I cannot imagine the pain you must have
endured—you and so many others whose loved ones have
given their lives in the service of their country. Last Veterans
Day, I addressed a Methodist congregation and told them
that we all owe an enormous debt of gratitude to the World
War II generation for what they did to defend freedom
around the world.

As to your question about greeting your loved ones in the
next world, I can think of no better reason to believe in the
hereafter than to read your letter and know that the very
nature of life demands it must continue after death.
Something in us lives on; that something is a spark of the
Divine, however imperfectly presented in its current form.
Because God is both good and all-powerful, your rendezvous
with those you love is as certain as tomorrow's sunrise.

But here is a secret about the future: When we pay attention to the present, the future takes care of itself. "Your
Father," said Jesus, "knows what you need before you ask
him" (Matthew 6:8). Unity emphasizes daily stillness in the
presence of God, which gives us the deepest assurance and
peace of mind about the future. It is in the present, in silent
communion with God, that we come to experience and
glimpse the reality of eternal life.

Dear Tom: Do you believe our state of mind/spirit affects where we go in an afterlife? How do you view the afterlife? What label would you put on it?
— **L.M., Columbia, South Carolina**

Dear L.M.: Coincidentally—if you believe in coincidences—I have been pondering this for quite some time now. Maybe it's because I'm middle-aged, and now the shadows of life draw long across my world, the night of death looms larger. The afterlife is probably a misnomer. If we are eternal beings, life runs continuously. Since our state of mind in this life influences the way we experience life in this world, it is likely that our state of mind will continue to influence our experience as we go onward. But I don't really know. I have said before in this space that I believe we cannot know anything of significance about what follows life in the physical plane.

You can buy books that display graphic illustrations of the floor plans in the Heavenly City; volumes have been "channeled" from beyond the veil; prophets of every religion offer visions that describe everything from ivory palaces to rivers of flame. Pardon me, but I flatly reject all such "special revelations" as the speculative daydreams of imaginative souls who, like all of us, want to know the unknowable.

As I am writing this—another coincidence?—on my stereo is Unity vocalist Carrie Norman singing "God Will Take Care" from the *Centennial Celebration: Carrie Norman Sings Songs of Unity* album. That is entirely the point. We can't know what awaits us after death. So like a blindfolded plank walker, we step off and trust that the depths will embrace us.

Therefore, behold the Christ in each person. Behold the footprints of God across the beauty of the world. Behold the goodness of creation. Behold the world as God must have envisioned it 15 billion years ago in the dark before the Big Bang. And the cosmic smile has not faded from God's face since that first glimpse of Truth so long ago. Behold the good, everywhere, and trust that whatever comes next will offer continuity with all which has come before it.

Dear Tom: For more than 50 years, I have been a seeker. New Thought/Unity seems to satisfy me the most. Their principles seem to help many people's health, happiness and prosperity problems. However, as we grow old most of us will become feeble, sicken and die. The only consolation seems to be a vague form of eternal life. Your thoughts would be appreciated.
— **D.C., Haddon Heights, New Jersey**

Dear D.C.: You know, I was just discussing this topic last week with one of the truly great teachers of the Unity movement, Rev. Tom Thorpe, who teaches in the Spiritual Education and Enrichment department of Unity Institute. We both acknowledged, as men now 60-plus years old, that the immortality we assumed without question in our youth has now become increasingly real and personal as the dark wall of death approaches in the far distance.

Even believing, as most people do, in an eternal life filled with light and joy—nevertheless, *living* a life span is far more concrete and intimate than believing in an abstract concept glibly called *eternal life*. My whole baby-boom generation, like all generations before and after, will one day end, which describes an organic, personalized experience. Merely believing in God is no stop against the angst of that approaching darkness. Even faithful people become frightened sometimes, and that encounter provides the point of growth from fear to greater faith.

Without having absolute knowledge about what awaits in eternity, there are some comforting indicators along the journey. Life has been good, full of people to love, and opportunities to learn and create. Why would eternity behave any differently? Have not most of the great prophets and teachers of humanity assured humanity that God has everything under control, backward and forward in time? Not just the established yesterdays and direct experiences of today, but God's presence and power journey with us into the unknown future, where a creative, developing existence requires ongoing consciousness for continued growth. Is not the meaning of faith and trust that, absent good evidence or absolute proof, we believe God is Absolute Good, and absolutely trustworthy?

To take life seriously in this world, we really must face the dark wall, which Shakespeare called the "unseen country" beyond life. But somehow in our souls we know the wall has another side ... For my generation, I hope it will be said that we walked into the darkness with faces turned to the light. As for me, I will go out with joy.

Let's get together in about a thousand years, somewhere in this cosmos or another, and discuss it further ... what do you say?

Dear Tom: My question may seem silly, but to me it is very important. My dear husband passed away on July 12, 1994. I miss him terribly. My question is, Will I meet him again when I die? Is there any passage in the Bible that I could read that would help me find the answer I'm looking for? Thank you.
— **J.C., Kenmore, New York**

Dear J.C.: There's nothing silly about your question at all. Your continuing love for your husband should be an inspiration to all couples. Love for a lifetime is possible if you both make a commitment and both are willing to work at it. And let me assure you: if anybody is entitled to spend eternity together, people like you and your husband will be first in line for a cottage somewhere in heaven.

In the New Testament we have Jesus promising Martha that "Those who believe in me, even though they die, will live, and everyone who lives and believes in me will never die" (John 11:25-26). My favorite passage refers to life after death has been demolished:

> Then I saw a new heaven and a new earth; for the
> first heaven and the first earth had passed away,
> and the sea was no more. And I saw the holy city,

the new Jerusalem, coming down out of heaven from God, prepared as a bride adorned for her husband. And I heard a loud voice from the throne saying, "See, the home of God is among mortals. He will dwell with them; they will be his peoples, and God himself will be with them; he will wipe every tear from their eyes. Death will be no more; mourning and crying and pain will be no more, for the first things have passed away."[3]

Dear Tom: My beautiful 29-year-old daughter, Krystal, was killed on December 10, 2003. She and her husband were bringing their 1-year-old twin sons home from a doctor's visit when a drunk driver slammed into their minivan and killed Krystal. My grief is beyond words. I would have gladly given my life to save hers, but I was not given the chance. Where is my daughter? Is she happy? I cannot imagine her being happy without her twin sons. She tried for seven years to have them, and then she had only one year of life to enjoy them. Why was she taken from her sons and not allowed to live her life? I feel that she was cheated out of her life. Will I ever be with my sweet baby again? I feel

like I am living in a nightmare without my daughter in this world.

— J.A., via Internet

Dear J.A.: I am at a loss for words as I reread your heartbreak-
ing letter. No one has fathomed the depths of grief like a parent who loses a child. There are no easy answers to the "why"
questions which invariably arise when tragedy takes someone so young and full of life. There are, however, certain spiritual thoughts which some have found comforting—God's
love is endless; God's light and joy extend beyond the dark
night of the soul to the brightness of an eternal communion in
which God-consciousness replaces fear and sadness.

Look to the story of Jesus in Gethsemane; meditate on the
light which came after his time of darkness, grief and pain.
Death has no power over your daughter because, like Jesus,
she is a radiant, spiritual being. We who stand on this side of
death's door have ample reason for tears and doubts, yet the
collective wisdom of the prophets and mystics of humanity
offers us hope for life which never ends. Near-death experiences and visionary encounters support the ancient dream of
a good eternity, but that door is in place and we cannot know
for sure. This lack of certainty is a blessing in disguise, precisely because we need to take this life seriously and do the
work that's ours to do, regardless of the obstacles, regardless
of how much it may hurt to go on sometimes.

Peace will come. Joy will return. Good memories will out-
last the wounds of sudden loss. And even though it may not
feel like it—even Jesus wondered if he had been forsaken—
God will, in fact, be with you every step of the way, just as

surely as Krystal walks in the light of the Divine Presence now and forever.

Special Note to Readers: I don't ordinarily step out of this column's natural music to make editorial noise, but listen carefully while I clang the loudest bell I can find, the fire alarm in your conscience. If you ever had any doubts about how important it is to prevent intoxicated men and women from driving motor vehicles, read J.A.'s heart-wrenching letter again. Better yet, read it aloud to your family. Send copies of the letter to your friends, especially anyone with a drinking problem. And do not let your friends, family—anyone whom you can reasonably prevent—ever drive drunk again. Unfortunately, no one can bring Krystal back to her grief-stricken mother, but perhaps we can keep another mother from suffering the devastating loss which J.A. has endured. Will you affirm the following prayer-pledge with me?

> *In memory of Krystal and all who have suffered because of drunk drivers, I pledge this day never to drive drunk and never to allow anyone to drive drunk if I can reasonably prevent it. With God's power, I see the roadways and streets clear of all danger. God's wisdom, light and protection embrace everyone who travels and make the highways safe now.*

Dear Tom: I prayed and prayed for my mother to live, but she died. Now I feel like "Truth" isn't really true. What did I do wrong? How can I get my faith back?

— C.T., Georgia (no city provided)

Dear C.T.: That's a tough one. You've suffered a loss, and you probably feel outraged, angry, hurt. After all, if we're trying to live the Jesus Christ teachings, shouldn't we be able to out-picture perfect health forever? Shouldn't we be able to help others overcome any disease? You might even feel betrayed by God. Of course, you know it isn't so. Otherwise, you wouldn't be asking for your faith back again.

Most of us feel these frustrations sometimes. A wise minister helped me after the death of a beloved church member by reminding me that death can be healing too. Sometimes, it's time to move on. Maybe you didn't do anything "wrong"— maybe your prayers helped your mother more than you'll know on this side. It isn't your job to know everything. Your job is to walk by the light you are given, trust God no matter what happens, and believe that God's goodness will prevail. *Less* than that will not be helpful. *More* than that is not required.

Good Questions

-17-

Forgiveness

Dear Tom: How can forgiveness be genuine when there is no repentance from the other party? Your answers, for the most part, are very informative. I thank you for any response I might receive.
— **G.F., Emporia, Kansas**

Dear G.F.: Forgiveness has nothing to do with the mental state of the other party. It is an act of supreme self-interest. We forgive because to do otherwise is to condemn ourselves to a self-made hell. Bitterness, envy, jealousy, malice and anger—all the traits of a personality in turmoil—flow from lack of forgiveness. To refuse to forgive is to choose misery. If the other party has truly wronged you and rejects any responsibility for the offense, forgiveness is your best defense against further suffering. Through forgiveness you begin a new pattern of relationships with others that puts you in control of your own consciousness.

Try this affirmation: *I behold the Christ in (name). I bless, release and forgive (name) for anything and everything that has happened.* When you can say that with conviction, add this: *(name) blesses, releases and forgives me as well.*

And remember—you don't have to approve of people's behavior to forgive them and to affirm that the Christ spirit dwells within them.

Dear Tom: Why is it so difficult to release and forgive negatives of the past? We think we have; then the same thing happens, and we're back into the past again.
— **Anonymous, Jonesboro, Georgia**

Dear Anonymous: If I asked for a show of hands out there, I wouldn't be surprised if most of our readers could have asked that question. Spiritual progress is part roller coaster, part treadmill. Every "zoom" seems to have its corresponding "blah." Perhaps you never really forgave and released "negatives of the past," or perhaps their roots run too deep for a single dose of metaphysical weed killer. I have found that repetition of affirmative prayer works best when treating recurring conditions, but you might need special counseling with a Unity minister or some work with a spiritually oriented psychologist. This is the important point: Don't give up! You can overcome any malaise of the mind, body or spirit with persistence and faith.

Dear Tom: In the Lord's Prayer, it says, "Forgive us our debts as we forgive our debtors." Now I find it interesting that in this prayer we ask God to forgive us. How can God forgive us for anything when God does not judge us?

— **L.N., Santa Rosa, California**

Dear L.N.: First, let's get the quote right: "And forgive us our debts, as we also have forgiven our debtors" (Matthew 6:12). Did you notice the tense of the verb in the second phrase? Forgiveness has already occurred. If we have forgiven those who wronged us, does this not suggest that God has already forgiven us for the corresponding offenses we have committed? When did all this forgiving take place? Perhaps Jesus is saying here that God wants us to turn the equation around and forgive the way God does—never to hold a grudge to begin with!

Another way to look at this passage is to see it as an affirmation of forgiveness rather than a supplication for it. Any way you turn it, I agree with you. God cannot "forgive" today what God has not "forgiven" yesterday, because God doesn't judge or hold a grudge. If we are doing things that impede our spiritual growth (that is, if we sin), does this make God angry, so that we need to win back God's approval? Isn't the act of wandering from the best path punishment enough? Why should God need to forgive me for acting the fool? The Divine within me knows I'll do it again and again, until I get it right sometime in the distant, endless future.

But let's not completely dismiss the idea of divine forgiveness. Sometimes my human mind needs reassurance; sometimes I feel so bad about things I've said or done (or left unsaid and undone) that I need to be reminded of God's never-ending love for me. And although I know intellectually that God isn't a stern Judge, I still need to kneel at the altar in prayer and whisper, "Father, forgive me." I hope you'll forgive me that vestige of an ancient way of thought.

Dear Tom: I've always wondered about the term "grace." Most Christians toss it around as if they assume everybody knows what it means, but I haven't a clue. What is the "grace of God?"
— M.C., Atlanta, Georgia

Dear M.C.: *Grace* is usually defined as an occasion when God does something for us that we don't expect, often something good that we don't feel we deserve. One could argue that this popular understanding of grace is based on a theological misunderstanding. God does nothing for us special, because God's goodness, "grace," is always available. Blessings, peace and wisdom come our way in proportion to our capacity to receive. We come into a world we did not create, ruled by forces beyond our control, and we seek supernatural assistance when life gets tough or scary. But that's not what we need. Not an interventionist God who reaches into time and space to rescue us, but a divine companion who walks the path with us, reminding us of the inner strength we have as children of God. All of us are the Christ.

Sometimes grace is linked to forgiveness, as in one of the best-known Christian hymns, written by Anglican clergyman John Newton (1725–1807):

Amazing Grace, how sweet the sound,
That saved a wretch like me.
I once was lost but now am found,
Was blind, but now I see.

The courage of the hymnists failed them when assembling the current edition of *Wings of Song*. It was an easy compromise to substitute *soul* for *wretch* in the first line of Newton's masterpiece. And who could blame them? I have heard people grousing that they refuse to sing the original wording because they aren't *wretches*. The same people cheerfully sing "We Three Kings" at Christmas without ever having ridden a camel. All right. Granted. You are not a wretch, and neither was John Newton. But as a former captain of a slave ship, Newton *felt* like a wretch, until his faith in Jesus Christ lifted the burden from him. That, my friends, is *grace*, and it's truly *amazing*.

If you have lived very long on planet Earth, there have doubtless been moments in your life when you have felt wretched too. All sentient beings have within them the power to achieve mastery over life's challenges, not by manipulating the world but by choosing how we shall respond to whatever happens. Although we do well to acknowledge the errors we make—how else can I learn unless my mistakes are faced honestly?—nevertheless, God doesn't need to forgive us, as Eric Butterworth has said, because He was never angry with us in the first place. The Christ dwells within each person; if grace exists, speak of the flash of insight that occurs when human consciousness realizes its divine potential. There grace abounds. Nothing else is required.

◌

Dear Tom: I have a question regarding Unity's view on salvation by grace through faith in Jesus Christ. Unity's literature seems to acknowledge it in a subtle way by saying that in order to become our best selves, it is necessary to turn from error to Truth and to acknowledge the divine in us and around us. This question has troubled me for sometime. Your perspective on it would be greatly appreciated.

— **J.B., St. Charles, Missouri**

Dear J.B.: You answered your own question, and quite well. For me, Jesus is the place in Western spiritual history where the Infinite, all-powerful God of the cosmos becomes focused in a finite life. When I look at Jesus of Nazareth, I glimpse through a window at something so vast that my mind can't grasp It. Without Jesus, I would not know what God is like and, consequently, what it means to be fully human.

Do others come to this knowledge without Jesus? Absolutely. I have no doubt that God has children in a million other worlds, none of whom have heard of Jesus, but who have certainly established an ongoing relationship with Divine Mind. Closer to home, I am also certain that God has spoken through other prophets, teachers and masters. But as a confessing Christian, the window I see God through is shaped like Jesus Christ. It is by grace that I have been born in the vicinity of that window and by faith that I have accepted its vision of the Truth. I don't know if that settles the problem for you, but it works for me.

-18-
Healing

Dear Tom: Pain, excruciating pain—why must some people experience it prior to dying? Why can't we go into a peaceful sleep and pass on? My mother passed away last year at the age of 63. She was very healthy all her life. Less than three months prior to her death she was diagnosed with lung cancer although she never smoked. The continuous, chronic pain that she endured for those three months should never have been. I am still angry and confused as to why a loving God would inflict this on a woman who was nothing less than a living saint all her life. She was a loving wife and mother of four children, a friend to many, and a person who exemplified the Christian/Unity way of life. Why did she have to suffer? I have searched for months and cannot come to terms with this. I would appreciate your insight.

— N.W. (no city/state provided)

Dear N.W.: Your question is the one I'm most frequently asked, so you're in good company. The usual pastoral advice about "affirming the good in every situation" often sounds like patronizing nonsense to someone who's hurting as much as you are, so I won't say that. Instead, let's cut to the hard truth: It's okay to be angry with God. It's okay to feel life makes no sense whatsoever. It's okay to scream at the ceiling, *"Where were You when I needed You?"*

God can take it. God won't get angry. God understands.

Plenty of us have felt moral outrage when someone we love has suffered. It is not a sign of weakness to question your faith.

I asked a priest once how to deal with sorrow and the suffering of the world. He was a highly spiritual person—some might call him a holy man. He smiled and said, "Look to the wounds of Jesus." I didn't like that answer. Actually, I didn't understand it. I thought he meant, "Jesus can solve all your problems." What he really meant, I believe, was that God is intimately involved in the suffering of every living thing. God is inside, not outside. God feels it all, works through it all.

Healing does not necessarily mean bodily health in a worldly sense—although it can mean this. Healing means harmony with God's flow of good. From your description, there is no doubt your mother received her healing: like Jesus, she achieved spiritual mastery in the face of a great physical challenge before being released from the struggle by death, which can be another form of healing. This is a metaphysical idea requiring much meditation and prayer, but I believe it is the key to the problem. God does not measure success by human standards. The mystical symbol of the cross suggests that God's power and presence are most powerfully present at moments of utter helplessness and despair. Jesus was despised by men, rejected by his own people, abandoned by his friends and followers, then left to die alone in agony. Yet through this one man's death, all humanity learned God is more powerful than death; Good Friday led straight to Easter—weakness became ultimate power, defeat became triumph, death became eternal life. This metaphysical Truth stands at the heart of the New Testament message, and its true significance has been undiminished after 20 centuries of human suffering.

Your mother chose to be the great, spiritual woman she was. Spirituality was not forced upon her by some divine program running in God's computer banks. She waded into the stream of life and lived it triumphantly. And the price we pay for the opportunity to choose the best path is that we must live in a cosmos where incomprehensible atrocities like this can happen to people who don't deserve them. In his book *On Being a Christian*, progressive Catholic theologian Hans Küng says if we believe God exists:

> Then, against all threats of emptiness and mean-
> inglessness, I could justifiably affirm the truth
> and significance of my existence: for God would
> be the ultimate meaning also of my life.[1]

I don't know if these words are helpful, but I leave you with one further thought. Our true nature is Spirit, and Spirit doesn't get sick. Our eternal destination is Oneness with God, even though the road may lead through the valley of the shadow. Your mother is beyond the shadow now, in the bright sunlight, surrounded by God's light and love.

Dear Tom: Doesn't metaphysical Christianity teach that good health is our divine right, assuming we believe and accept the gift? If so, what about James Dillet Freeman's wife, Billie, who died of Alzheimer's disease, and the Reverend Peggy Basset, pastor of a Religious Science church in California, who succumbed to Lou Gehrig's disease? If people of great faith and prayer are felled by such horrible diseases, what chance or hope is there for a poor, dumb schlemiel like me?
— **J.B., Los Angeles, California**

Dear J.B.: First, you are not a schlemiel, and second, you've raised a common question: Why do bad things happen to good people? Except you've given it an interesting spin that I'd like to address here—Why do bad things happen to persons of great faith and prayer? If they're doing the right thing, spiritually, shouldn't they be immune? The following answer, like all the comments in this column, reflects one theologian's viewpoint—mine. But, that's what you're asking for, so here goes. We are not immune to the foibles of life, no matter how spiritual we are. Life experiences show us this fact.

I think we need to stop thinking out of the Newtonian model of the universe and start thinking quantum physics. I believe Truth principles are just that—principles—not absolute laws motivated by cause and effect. If we affirm health, happiness and prosperity, we will tend to be healthier, happier and more prosperous. Yet the everyday events of life show us that we can't reliably predict things which are as complex as the inner workings of the spiritual/metaphysical cosmos, nor can we predict the pathway of any individual human being, no matter how spiritually accomplished he or she may be. No matter what the appearance, you cannot know the individual challenges a person is meeting along his or her own path.

You mentioned two spiritual people and asked how *they* could have suffered. Perhaps we might reflect on why the most spiritual person of all, Jesus Christ, suffered and died. Metaphysical Christians believe it was to show us the Way, but the way to what? To some sort of exalted-guru mastery, so that no "bad" thing can happen? Or to Christ consciousness, so that no matter what happens, we can know that God is good, life is good, and in God everything is working together for that good? Everyone's pathway to God is unique. Jesus suffered crucifixion, but the outcome was resurrection.

Your question is an ancient one, and I'm under no illusion that I've answered it to anyone's total satisfaction.

Dear Tom: How much relief from illness can be possibly achieved through prayer work, regularly attending services, spiritual meditation and tithing? I have been diagnosed with clinical depression. I currently take medication for it, which works some of the time. I have been intrigued with the idea of divine healing, especially with how Myrtle Fillmore achieved her healing. Although I am now retired, for most of my life I have had to deal with this very serious illness. I believe I have now found the dimension in my life that has been sorely missing. Can I be healed?

— **J.H., Orlando, Florida**

Dear J.H.: Yes! And both medical science and spiritual science can play roles, because all healing comes from the same source. I would not counsel someone to abandon medicine the way Myrtle did, coming home from the lecture by E.B. Weeks and throwing out all the bottles which had accrued in her bathroom cabinet. She had tuberculosis—*consumption,* as they called it in the 19th century—and often that was tantamount to a death sentence. The state of the medical arts in those days was so primordial that she probably did herself a favor by chucking the elixirs and potions prescribed by her doctors.

However, today's medical science is often nothing short of a miracle of God. Even so, the old Unity maxim remains valid: "Go first to God, then to man (or woman) as God directs." So I would recommend a two-pronged attack on the problem; that is, spiritual centering and medical treatment. Contact your local Unity minister for more information on prayer techniques, denials and affirmations, and positive image meditations. Medical science is becoming more aware all the time that healing has a dimension which goes beyond the physical, which is the very definition of metaphysical Christian faith.

Dear Tom: I am confused about the things I read about healing—the idea that all physical illness can be healed with prayer—and the very obvious reality of our mortality and that eventually every last one of us is going to die of something, no matter how "spiritual" or "prayerful" each of us is. Could you shed some light on this seeming contradiction? I know I'm missing something!
— **B.P., Los Angeles, California**

Dear B.P.: I know what you mean. Work all your life to get spiritually in tune, but you die anyway. My other California friends might call that a "spiritual bummer." And so it might be—if death were the end, not simply the next phase of life. As my generation (baby boomers) grows older, we're facing death with mixed reactions. Some become more intensely religious—to the point of flights into fundamentalism. Others reject all religion and decide to play harder while daylight still shines in their skies. But we know our generation's sun is setting, and we know the hour will come when we have to go home for the night.

The real question isn't, How long can we stave off death? The question we should be asking is: How can we live most effectively in the life that we have before us? It is a fundamental principle that by focusing on the present and the spiritual growth you are making now, the future will take care of itself. I believe one answer will suffice: Follow the model of Jesus Christ, the Way Shower and Savior (also *Healer*, same word in Greek). And what was that model? As Paul put it: "Christ in you, the hope of glory" (Colossians 1:27). The Christ is the divine potential in every person.

So love one another, strive for justice, practice kindness, lavish forgiveness upon everyone, and be a healing influence. Prayer does heal, because prayer tunes us to the life of God. But healing, while it may include physical restoration, is always more. Whether physical healing occurs or not, real healing is your oneness with God.

Dear Tom: Our church has begun hands-on healing practices and has attracted new people who are interested in this ancient tradition. There is even talk of establishing a "healing room" for laying on of hands at the church. What do you think about "healing touch" and hands-on healing?
— T.D., Los Angeles, California

Dear T.D.: Anything that works is a blessing, but I go with the tradition which, through the years, has stressed the mental/spiritual aspects of healing instead of physical contact. The reason some healers took this hands-off view is simply that physical touch introduces elements of human ego into the healing process—namely, the personality and physical self of the counselor—which can easily be misinterpreted, misconstrued, misjudged by the one searching for healing. It is something to keep in mind.

Even though some people seem to have a "gift" for healing by touch, I have always believed there really are no special gifts—just specially developed people. We all have the Christ within us. Each person is equally powered and with the right mental attitude will become equally powerful. How can there be more divinity in one person or place than another? Look at the biblical accounts of healing.

Jesus touched some people, but with others he simply said the word and the healing was accomplished. He often followed acts of healing with the declaration "Your faith has made you well" (Matthew 9:22). This is the key. Spiritual healing is never forced upon someone; a person must believe, and believing alone is sufficient.

All healing comes from within, not from the outside. Even medicine, which is another form of divine healing, heals from within by assisting the body in healing itself. "Laying on of hands" can suggest a superior-inferior relationship between a healer and victim. We are not victims; we are the powerful daughters and sons of a loving, supportive, health-empowering God. Personally, I prefer the tradition of spiritual and mental healing alone, without the necessity for hands-on contact.

Dear Tom: Do you believe in doctors, or do you only rely on prayer?
— **A.L.D., San Diego, California**

Dear A.L.D.: The decision to seek medical aid is up to the individual. A principle that I learned early in my experiences with spiritual healing was "Go first to God, then to man as God directs." This is an old idea, as the gender-biased language reveals, but it is still valid. All healing comes from God, whether assisted by medicine or energized by prayer alone.

Dear Tom: Is it true that Unity co-founder Charles Fillmore was born with one leg shorter than the other and through faith was healed? I was told that the shorter leg grew.
— **Anonymous, via Internet**

Dear Anonymous: Charles Fillmore was not born with one leg shorter than the other. He was injured in a skating accident when he was 10 years old. Bedridden for two years while a raging infection attacked his hip, young Mr. Fillmore emerged from the experience with a withered, painful leg that required a brace. After Myrtle was healed from tuberculosis, Charles began to study spiritual healing. Over the years, his leg grew longer and stronger, the pain diminished, and he discarded the brace. He walked with a slight limp all his life, needing only a little extra shoe heel to compensate. You can read all about it in *The Story of Unity*, by James Dillet Freeman, available through any Unity bookstore and online at *unity.org*.

-19-
Prosperity

Dear Tom: I was raised in a traditional church that taught we should approach God wringing our hands and pleading, but this reduces us to the level of a helpless beggar and God becomes a tyrannical figure. At the opposite extreme, I have encountered the notion that, as human beings, we have a right to an endless supply of health and prosperity and that we need only affirm this to the Creator. While this is an attractive idea, I am not certain one should approach God with an attitude that seems presumptuous. What attitude should I adopt when approaching God in prayer?

— **T.V., San Francisco, California**

Dear T.V.: It is amazing how many people think of God is too holy to be approached and too serious to be friendly. Jesus looked at God as a parent and friend who "knows what you need before you ask him" (Matthew 6:8). For Jesus, "It is your Father's good pleasure to give you the kingdom" (Luke 12:32). Well, if it's God's "good pleasure" to give you the kingdom, shouldn't it be your "good pleasure" to accept it?

Of course, the way you approach God will depend upon your spiritual/emotional state when you pray. I agree that approaching God like a helpless beggar is not the best idea, but there have been times when I have felt so lowly that the words about the divine majesty of the psalms have been my only solace (Psalms 8, 51, 103 and 107 are especially good). But if I'm serious about accepting that "kingdom" which God so freely gives, I'll keep in mind the affirmative approach to God. My all-time favorite verse for "how to approach God" is from Philippians 4:4-7, Paul's happiest letter:

> Rejoice in the Lord always; again I will say, Rejoice. Let all men know your forbearance. The Lord is at hand. Have no anxiety about anything, but in everything by prayer and supplication with thanksgiving let your requests be made known to God. And the peace of God, which passes all understanding, will keep your hearts and your minds in Jesus Christ.

Dear Tom: We are constantly discussing prosperity and the thought that God will always send us good. Now this I believe in a certain way—the spiritual way. Yes, God will help our consciousness and spiritual outlook. But to many people today, "prosperity" seems to always mean having worldly possessions. So often this prosperity talk is about a new car or house and so on. Yes, God is for the good of

God's people, but surely they must think of their faith and higher consciousness. I feel the spiritual outlook is so demanding, the rest will follow if our faith is firm.

— **P.F., Atlantic Beach, Florida**

Dear PF: Some letters require a page of response. Others— like yours—need only a hearty "Amen!"

Dear Tom: What can I do to increase prosperity in my life? Is it sinful to pray for wealth?

— **C.S., Chicago, Illinois**

Dear C.S.: Not so much sinful as ineffective. A better technique would be to affirm prosperity—to see yourself receiving all the good things that God wants you to enjoy. Prosperity to me doesn't mean having endless wealth, but having enough resources to comfortably do the things you need to do for effective living in this world and to live a balanced life. For some people, their balanced life requires great wealth; for others, perhaps a rather meager amount would suffice. Balance, harmony and spiritual growth are the goals, not economic muscle for its own sake.

To answer your implied question: No, it isn't wrong to want wealth, but it is "sinful" (that is, an error-belief which leads to spiritual dysfunction) either to live for money or feel powerless to overcome poverty. God's treasure-house has plenty of supply awaiting you. Open your mind and heart and prepare yourself to receive the good. For more guidance, try the book *DAILY WORD Prosperity*, a 90-day program of devotional messages to help build a consciousness of abundance and joy.

> Dear Tom: I have a concern about prosperity teachings. Our Western society is overly materialistic, causing too much resource consumption and harming of the environment. This could be helped by learning to seek spiritual fulfillment instead of pursuit of material things.
> — **R.K., Morgan Hill, California**

Dear R.K.: No argument here. We seek first the kingdom of God, and then all these things are added unto us. Not the other way around. I have always held that *prosperity is about quality, not quantity.* Some people need a million dollars to achieve harmony with life and the Divine; others would find the reality of great wealth to be a burden. What I like to visualize is a balanced life, where resources meet needs and promote spiritual, intellectual and interpersonal growth. However, I also believe prosperity teachings are needed today more than ever. You can grow spiritually in any circumstance, but few people find their highest potential released while carrying the weight of poverty.

Dear Tom: I'm 90 years old and probably much too wordy, but I don't know why it has always been believed that being poor is more God-like. Why must we believe that Jesus was a member of the peasant class, the son of a poor, uneducated carpenter? His mother, Mary, was cousin to Elizabeth, the wife of Zecharias, who was a member of the Abijah division of the Temple servers, certainly not from the peasant class. Was he educated? He knew and quoted the prophets; he read aloud and wrote in the dirt. There's a crying hunger in me for my fellow men to realize what a lovely person Jesus was. Certainly there's nothing wrong with peasants, but part of Jesus' astounding life that is completely overlooked is that he gave up a life of ease and comfort, as well as his life itself, for us.
— **C.L., Blanco, Texas**

Dear C.L.: I wish space had allowed me to reproduce the whole text of your excellent letter rather than summarizing the points after a little gentle editing, but I hope the above condensation does justice to your intent.

You're absolutely right when you say many people have a problem believing that wealthy individuals can also be spiritual. Some folks advocate this "holy poverty" nonsense by misquoting the Scripture. "The Bible teaches that money is the root of all evil," they insist. Actually, the Bible says something very different: "For the love of money is the root of all evils; it is through this craving that some have wandered away from the faith and pierced their hearts with many pangs" (1 Timothy 6:10).

Note that when people pursue wealth as their highest aspiration, it will "pierce their hearts." It is not wealth itself but the misplaced focus on acquisition that causes the problems. Although it is a bit of a stretch to see Jesus as well-to-do, even by ancient standards, nevertheless some of the greatest spiritual leaders in human history have been, to use Charles Fillmore's term, millionaires. We could list biblical characters like Moses (who was raised as Pharaoh's son); Jacob (who held vast flocks); Jacob's son Joseph (who commanded the storehouses of Egypt, which was the greatest economic and military power in the Near East at the time); wealthy and powerful Hebrew kings like David and Solomon; the prophet Nehemiah (a member of the inner circle of the King of Persia); and Esther (Queen of Persia). All of these persons were Old Testament millionaires! To the list we could add affluent New Testament characters like Zacchaeus, Joseph of Arimathea, the apostle Matthew, and prosperous Romans like Philemon. In modern times, even a selfless figure like Mother Teresa, working among the destitute and sick street people of Calcutta, needed to keep the contributions pouring in to keep life-giving, hope-inspiring activities alive.

Not only Christian and Jewish millionaires have found the path to spiritual enlightenment: Buddha and Baha'u'llah were wealthy princes; Mohammed's wife, Kadijah, was quite rich. All his life, Confucius vainly sought an appointment among the provincial rulers of China, but his teachings, which encouraged all people to aspire to the highest attributes of society, may have displeased the Chinese nobility and thus prevented him from receiving their patronage. Or maybe his prosperity consciousness attracted the perfect circumstance to Confucius, that is, the life of an itinerant teacher who would leave the world richer by his moral and ethical sayings.

I would say that Jesus was probably neither a penniless urchin nor a land-owning aristocrat, but a relatively prosperous tradesman (carpenter, a.k.a., house builder). He learned to read and write—like Jewish boys have done throughout history—so he could study the Torah. I doubt that he was a millionaire, but it is likely that he had a good childhood in Nazareth and the nearby Hellenized Jewish city of Sepphoris.

Dear Tom: I remember one Bible verse my mom would always say: "God helps those who help themselves." I do everything that I can physically do, but it seems like it is never enough! I can't seem to earn enough to meet my monthly obligations let alone save for a rainy day or have the money to help others in need. What else can I do except pray? Your feedback is very much appreciated!
— **D.K., Maybee, Michigan**

Dear D.K.: My dear, you could greatly benefit from a good course in prosperity principles. Call a Unity Church nearby—there are plenty of them in Michigan! Meanwhile, I recommend Catherine Ponder's works, especially *Open Your Mind to Prosperity*, the book that changed my life. And by the way, the quote "God helps those who help themselves" isn't from the Bible; it's attributed to Benjamin Franklin.

Dear Tom: Maybe you have answered this question before, but one of the few things that bothers me about New Thought is its emphasis on prosperity. I can't help be bothered by programs and books that directly or indirectly emphasize the accumulation of wealth (e.g., "Millionaire Mind"). How can I think about my current prosperity in light of the suffering in the world around me? In the USA and many other counties there are programs to provide for people's basic needs for food and shelter. But much of the world does not have this available. They watch their children starve. If I were a missionary working in Darfur, I would be hard pressed to offer only an attitude adjustment. My concern for these people would call from me material gifts of food and medicine to meet these basic needs. As I ponder this, two thoughts come to mind: 1) I remember the story (from *Chicken Soup for the Soul*) of the person on a beach that was covered in washed up starfish, throwing them one at a time back into the water. He was criticized that he could

not fix the whole problem; he could not throw all the starfish back. He countered after heaving a starfish into the water, "Well, it made a difference to that one." 2) New Thought provides a foundational change that might prevent the political problems that caused Darfur. Your thoughts?
— **K.J.E., via Internet**

Dear K.J.E.: My thought is: *I love it when someone answers his own question!* But I wouldn't send missionaries to convert the heathen, perhaps because I rather *like* heathens. I'd like to think we respect the indigenous religious traditions of every land and culture as paths to God, however defined. And yet, as you suggest, New Thought people tend to believe the principles of prosperity thinking will work in any context, no matter how alien or drastic those circumstances may seem.

Others are catching the vision too. One of the most visible is the smiling young televangelist, Joel Osteen, who arguably preaches metaphysical Christianity, with a slightly conservative twist, to his huge congregation and to millions via syndicated TV shows and best-selling books:

> If you don't develop the habit of expecting good things to come your way, then you're not likely to receive anything good. If you don't expect things to get better, they probably won't. If all you expect is more of the same, that's all you're going to have. Our expectations set the boundaries for our lives.[1]

Yes, spiritual principles will work in Darfur. When people begin to believe in the God-power working within and through them, dynamic forces are released that can lift anyone, anywhere, out of poverty consciousness and set them on the road to prosperity.

-20-
Odds and Ends

Dear Tom: Please give me a definition of Truth. Sincere thanks for your help on my spiritual journey.

— **J.W., Montville, New Jersey**

Dear J.W.: Charles Fillmore, who is one of my favorite systematic theologians and mystical thinkers, gave a brilliant answer to your question:

> Truth—The Absolute; that which accords with God as divine principle; that which is, has been, and ever will be; that which eternally is. The Truth of God is reality: "the same yesterday and today, *yea* and for ever." The verities of being are eternal and have always existed. Truth abides in fullness at the very core of man's being. As his consciousness (awareness) expands, he touches the everlasting Truth. What seems new is but the unveiling of that which always has been.[1]

The good you seek is already here, as the eternal Truth of God. For example, you may be ill in body, but at "the very core" of your being is health. Or you may be experiencing the lack of a job and prosperity, but at "the very core" of your being is the power to prosper you. The power of Truth in this absolute sense is that it lies beyond the facts we see every day and draws us ever onward to greater life, health and abundance. Paying attention to this absolute Truth does not mean that we ignore the facts in our lives. Absolute Truth simply points us beyond the facts to explore new possibilities and realize the true depth of our potential.

> Dear Tom: My life is a mess. My marriage is loveless. My children don't listen to me. I'm overweight and can't make my money stretch to the end of the month. Unity refers to itself as "practical" Christianity. What is there in Unity to help somebody like me?
> — **P.W., Seattle, Washington**

Dear P.W.: Start by taking a deep breath and saying out loud: *I am the perfect child of God, filled with wisdom, peace and light.* Say it, no matter how foolish you feel. Don't believe it? Of course you don't believe it! Nobody believes it—at least, not at first. That's why we repeat affirmations again and again. We need to redirect a lifetime of thinking—shock ourselves out of our spiritual lethargy—with positive thoughts to replace all the junk we've been taught about how worthless we are.

Next, since you are God's child, quietly seek God's presence each day. The truth is that there is only One Presence and One Power in your life, and when there are problems you can't handle, God can handle them. In fact, take time to actually see God working to transform your life.

Next, find a quiet place each day to affirm your prosperity, to say aloud what a wonderful, joy-filled, prosperous person you are. And don't stop with yourself. Affirm good things about the people in your world who are driving you crazy—your husband, your children, your creditors, anybody! See them surrounded by God's light, love and peace and showered by an endless flow of abundance.

Will this make your marriage a Hollywood romance movie? Will it put a million dollars in your bank account or get your kids accepted into Harvard? Actually, it could ... but what matters more is that it will *definitely* have some kind of positive effect in your life, affairs and relationships. Affirm the good, and you will see more good out-pictured in your life. Will this solve all your problems? Probably not overnight, but you know how many steps it takes to begin a journey of one thousand miles, don't you?

> Dear Tom: If not Christianity, what religion would you follow?
> — **D.E., Monterey, California**

Dear D.E.: Now that's an original one! Let s see—I find good insights in so many places ... I love Judaism, but that's cheating. Too close to Christianity. Islam is fascinating, with its stress on purity of worship and world brotherhood. Hinduism has so many exciting spiritual practices. Buddhism has the noble eightfold path, and I have great Buddhist friends, like the venerable Bhante Wimala.[2] But I think if I weren't a Christian I'd probably be a Bahá'í.

Just as Christianity emerged from Jewish roots, the Bahá'í Faith originated as a sect of Islam in the mid-1800s, inspired by the teachings of the 19th-century Persian prophet, Bahá'u'lláh. Today the Bahá'í Faith is an independent religion found in practically every community around the globe. Bahá'ís believe in the oneness of humanity, the essential unity of all religions, and the equality of men and women. Followers of Bahá'u'lláh are required to pray daily—something I think Christians should imitate—and are forbidden from consuming intoxicants. And the voluminous Bahá'í religious writings are absolutely beautiful.[3]

Truth comes in many packages. Those of us who have been born into the Christian worldview have the challenge to find Truth both within our heritage and in the wisdom of other traditions. To do this with neither compromise nor bigotry is the challenge of this new era of global awareness.

Dear Tom: I want to use the Bible more in my devotional life. Can you suggest some spiritual exercises that are both thoroughly Unity and based on biblical texts?
— **S.M., Vermont (no city provided)**

Dear S.M.: Oh, yes. The Bible is a marvelous place to explore with your divine-human power of imagination. Find a biblical setting that appeals to you—Mount Sinai (with or without Charlton Heston), the temple in Jerusalem, the palace of King David, the upper room where Jesus met with his disciples— and "walk into" the scene. Notice the smells, the textures of clothing, the feel of the rocky earth beneath your sandaled feet. Study the people and listen to their chatter, which you will understand because it's *your* imagination at work.

My two favorite scenes are the manger at Bethlehem and the lakeshore at Galilee. In the former, I sneak up behind the ox to watch the Magi unfold their treasures, then kneel and look for myself. In the other scene, I take a walk along the shore of first century Lake Galilee, where I find a crowd gathered to hear Jesus, who speaks from a fishing boat. I get into the crowd and listen. You'd be amazed what I hear, especially when he looks directly at *me*. Sometimes, if I'm very brave, I wait after the crowd disperses and stroll up to Jesus, and we take a walk along the shore together, talking. *And you can do it too.*

In these "Bible trips," you can just listen or ask questions; you'd be surprised what answers people have received! Of course, we know these excursions are trips within us, not some invading images projected from the supernatural. That's okay. I have always believed that God is to be found as near as inside us, yet fully present beyond the farthest star.

Dear Tom: I am a new Truth student and I have been wondering what your views are on topics such as the Sabbath, unclean meats, paradise, and Satan as the Evil One. Can you please explain?
— **G.H., St. Michael, Barbados**

Dear G.H.: Hebrew Scriptures declared that to be a faithful Israelite meant following certain practices and avoiding certain evils. The Sabbath was Saturday, and the faithful Jew still observes it from sunset Friday until sunset Saturday. In Unity we understand the spiritual Sabbath as the inner act of letting go and letting God. Also, pork products and quite a few other foods (shellfish and all other seafood without scales; snakes, lizards, insects and anything that creeps or crawls; certain birds and land animals) are taboo to the observant Jew. In Christian Scriptures, this rule is modified by Jesus and the first-century Christian community.

And now for Satan ... As you read the Bible in depth, it becomes clear that Satan serves as our personification of all the lowest elements in human character, as well as a convenient explanation for all the negative things we can't explain in any other way. We don't need a Satan hot from Hades. It is we humans who create our own hells and act like the very devil towards each other. We do, however, need a Way Shower and Redeemer to bring us the keys to the kingdom, to demonstrate that divine power which dwells within each of us.

Now the metaphysical Christian way is to meditate, pray and center yourself on the indwelling Christ. All of these interesting questions become trivial when standing on holy ground, where you will discover the "secret place of the most High" (Psalm 91:1 KJV) within your own consciousness. Read Psalm 96, 1 Corinthians 13, and the fourth chapter of Paul's letter to the Philippians. Then take a walk along those dazzling, white sand Barbados beaches and commune directly with the Christ within you.

Dear Tom: Why doesn't God speak to people today?
No book has been added to the Bible since the first
few Christian centuries. Is God dead?
— C.K., Georgia (no city provided)

Dear C.K.: That really is a good question! The best answer is that, like the works of Shakespeare, the biblical writings are completed. So are the *Bhagavad Gita, Talmud, Koran, Book of Mormon* and the letters of Myrtle Fillmore. *Completed* doesn't mean "closed"; it simply means "finished." After an inspired work is accomplished—and I use the word "inspired" in its most generous, most inclusive form—the role of the religious community changes from *creative* to *interpretive*. The community of faith which produced the Bible now turns its energies to interpreting this anthology of primordial memories for each new generation.

Properly understood, the task of biblical interpreters today is to help the ancient authors speak the language and symbolism of modern humanity. To do this, Jewish and Christian thinkers have published scholarly commentaries on the Scripture, but poets, playwrights and storytellers have also been at work reshaping the ancient themes, recasting the old dramas with modern faces.

What is *Jonathan Livingston Seagull*, if not a parody of the old prophetic story summarized by Jesus in Matthew's Gospel?

> And they took offense at him. But Jesus said to them, "Prophets are not without honor except in their own country and in their own house." [4]

But as inspired as *Jonathan Livingston Seagull* may appear to some readers, it remains an interpretation of biblical themes, not a candidate for the Bible. The musical *West Side Story* was a marvelous adaptation of *Romeo and Juliet*, but you won't find Tony and Maria in the next edition of Shakespeare's complete works.

The canon of Scripture was completed before any of us were born. Our task today is to find new ways to "tell the old, old story" for generations yet unborn. God is alive and well and speaking through us.

> Dear Tom: I don't know what to believe about psychics. I have read some of their books and have seen some of their work, and it appears that they are God-centered and are helping people. A friend of mine said they are really getting their information from the devil and that the Bible warns us about this in Acts 16, Leviticus 17 and Leviticus 20. However, the psychics I know are constantly assuring people that life is eternal and our souls pass on to the other side. How can what they do be considered evil or the work of an Antichrist?
> — **L.K., Magalia, California**

Dear L.K.: Your friend's concern for you is commendable, but she's looking at life from a perspective the late Carl Sagan critically analyzed in his book *The Demon-Haunted World*.

Some people do, in fact, believe the world is populated with evil spirits whose job skills include seducing innocent *souls* from truth by tempting *us* with a candy store window full of New Age practices. As I look out at the world, I see no evidence of evil spirits, just people making choices that sometimes lead to "evil" results.

Don't get me wrong. I agree with your friend in one respect: There are lots of eccentric New Age practices out there masquerading as religious truth. This is not exactly breaking news. Pick up one of those locally produced, free-for-the-asking newspapers in your region and you'll discover a Pandora's box of white magic, séances, assorted forms of paganism (Celtic, Earth Mother, Wiccan, etc.), astrology, psychics, voodoo (I'm serious!) and UFO devotions. These nontraditional activities vary along a wild and wide spectrum, from the innocuous and helpful group study of *A Course in Miracles* to the dangerous and sometimes illegal practices of black magic. I've probably made some readers angry in the past by taking a critical look at some of these exotic religious expressions. But none of them—not even Satanism—are "of the Devil" because there is no Devil out there to be *of*. (Did you follow that convoluted syntax?) Unity believes there is only One Presence and One Power in our lives and in the universe, God the good, Omnipotent. That doesn't leave a lot of wiggle room for the Devil or his friends in low places.

About psychics and the Bible ... Right, they are specifically discussed several times in Old and New Testament texts, but they are usually shown pretty favorably. Looking at the passages you mentioned, I find no mention of New Age practices in the Revised Standard Version translation of Leviticus 17, and Leviticus 20 refers to séances and black magic, not psychics. In Acts 16:16-20, the apostle Paul chases a spirit from a girl who was able to see the future but not because the spirit is evil or that the apostle disapproves of her profession. Paul was annoyed because she had followed them for days, screeching about their mission as servants of the Most High God. So he drove out the spirit to shut her up. Because she was a slave whose job skills were nullified, Paul got into trouble with her owners. Nothing in the passage is even slightly critical of psychic powers.

Actually, both the Old and New Testaments have God-centered people who are consulted to get readings about the fate of kings and kingdoms. One could make a plausible case that some of the prophets were used the way psychics are today. And didn't Pharaoh send for Joseph to interpret his dreams?

Personally, I avoid psychics. Not because they are bad people (they're not) but because visiting them is not the best spiritual practice. You have the power to find your own answers within, so why pay for a psychic reading when you can ask the Christ within you for free?

Dear Tom: Can you explain how Christ fits into Unity's philosophy? I have been raised a Christian and find the teachings of the Unity Church very helpful in my spiritual growth, but I am young in understanding the philosophy of Unity. It appears to me that Christ is not a central focus of Unity but a manifestation of God. Is he considered a teacher or actually our savior?

— W.Y., Sacramento, California

Dear W.Y.: Blessings to everyone in my beloved Sacramento! I joyfully served four years as senior minister at Sunrise Unity Church in the California capital. Now, to your question ...

I think a lot of New Thought people use the word *philosophy* when they really mean two other things: 1) *way of life* and 2) *theology*. Unity is *not* a philosophy; it is a system of theology in support of a way of life. Philosophy and theology differ in that philosophers theoretically have no beginning point but simply follow truth wherever it guides them. While this sounds like a good idea, it does not describe a community of faith, such as Judaism, Islam or Buddhism.

Theology starts within a circle of faith. Jews begin with the Torah and Talmud; Muslims affirm there is no God but God; Buddhists have the Noble Eightfold Path. A Jewish scholar may study Islam, a Buddhist may read the Book of Mormon, but they approach that endeavor wearing the lenses of faith they have acquired as participant members of a living religious tradition, and that is one of the elements in the definition of theology. A Unity minister starts with certain preconceived concepts; for example, that God is One Presence, One Power and Absolute Good. While there is nothing wrong with someone who believes otherwise, the Unity way begins *here*. We are flexible, but not shapeless.

What all that means, and how we should apply it to life, is the task of theology. Personally I am a deep believer in the centrality of Jesus Christ in Unity's theology, but I think it's fair to say that for some New Thought ministers, *Jesus* is not a central emphasis, although *the Christ* is, and it is this faith in the Christ that is universal to the metaphysical Christian way of life. Metaphysical Christianity sees Jesus the Christ as its central figure, however he may be understood. Unity separates the historical Jesus from the theological Christ, as do virtually all modern biblical scholars beyond the fundamentalist fringe.

Jesus of Nazareth was a man who lived, taught and died about 2,000 years ago. After his death at the hands of the Romans, many of his followers believed they still had access to him through visions, prayer and spiritual experiences. However, the *Christ* is not limited to the historical Jesus. The *Christ* refers to the indwelling divinity that animates every sentient being.

Life brings hope of growth toward Christ-consciousness. We are all incarnations of the Divine, struggling to realize our oneness with the Father-Mother God as completely as Jesus did. Life brings challenges, but even in the face of the worst that could happen, God is working through it all to bring perfect, long-term results. There really is only One Presence/Power, and the birth, life, teachings, death and resurrection of Jesus demonstrate how completely God's goodness will triumph over all appearances to the contrary.

To me, Christianity as taught by the Master is not an exclusive religion that says, "Nobody's going to heaven but the members of my church!" The biblical record shows a Jesus who met with people from all backgrounds, including non-believers and foreigners. Jesus the Christ showed us how the love of God looks when somebody actually lives it. So did other people, like Buddha, St. Francis of Assisi, Baha'u'llah, Mohandas Gandhi and Mother Teresa. Jesus provided a clear model of the God-directed life, albeit not the only model. That's why I am a follower of Jesus Christ and a Christian. That's why my theological understanding of the Christ guides me along the path to the Unity way of life.

Dear Tom: Do you think there is both a feminine and masculine side to God? Most Protestant faiths have a problem with this idea.
— D.V., Jordanville, New York

Dear D.V.: Oh, yes. Religious literature abounds with references to "Father-Mother God" and the feminine aspect of divinity. Actually, since God is spirit, the Divine is neither masculine nor feminine. But, as you rightly mention, male images of the Divine have dominated Protestant thought, and a corrective period of contemplation about God's feminine aspect might be in order. May I suggest a meditation exercise? See yourself cradled in the arms of the divine Mother God as She sings you a lullaby. It's an experience of divine love unlike any you've contemplated.

Dear Tom: I was wondering if Goddess-based spirituality is addressed or welcomed in your church. Raised in the Episcopal Church (my husband was raised in the Jewish faith), I have been following the Wiccan/Pagan path for about 10 years now and find that my devotion to Goddess fills my heart with love. I have always held great love for Jesus and his teachings but really disliked the dogma of the church that I grew up with.

My cousin attends the Unity Church of San Francisco. I live in the Sacramento area and enjoy hearing different speakers on different philosophies, but I don't like being told that I'm a heathen or someone who is going to hell! I don't believe in a hell per se. I believe that we are all connected to our mother Earth and that the Divine is made up of the God and Goddess.

I am pregnant and plan on raising my child on this path, but I wonder if your church is right for me. It is difficult to not have groups of people to share my beliefs with; many pagans are solitaries, and we don't really have a church to go to for our beliefs. I would appreciate any input and insight you might be able to give.

— **D.C., Sacramento, California**

Dear D.C.: First, let me say that you and I probably have a lot more in common than you realize. Unity doesn't believe in hell, either, and many of us prefer language like "Father-Mother God" when offering prayer. You say "the Divine is made up of the God and Goddess"—I say the Divine is made up of all consciousness, that the very intelligence by which you are reading and deciphering this string of incomplete thoughts I am sending your way is, in fact, Divine Mind in microcosm. As a Wiccan you will be welcome at any meta-physical church, and probably find that much of the program conformably fits your theology. Unity people generally like earth-based spirituality and weave those ideas into their other beliefs. We find it acceptable to refer to God in the female as well as male, since neither is correct and therefore equally valid as a symbol. Personally, I have enjoyed close friendships with Wiccans. When I lived Georgia, I attended Wiccan holiday gatherings like Samhain and Yule.

Having said that, let me say that Unity is a metaphysical *Christian* denomination, but not in the usual, pejorative sense of the word. We represent tolerant, inclusive Christianity, the kind that Jesus taught. (See any of Bishop John Shelby Spong's books for an Episcopal view on inclusive Christianity.) We are not into anyone dying for our sins. Jesus is to Christianity as Buddha is to Buddhism—the way-shower, guide, teacher, guru. If inclusive Christianity appeals to you, just show up Sunday at any Unity church. You'll find a nice pool of fellow heretics to wade into!

Dear Tom: I have attended a nice church for several years, but now we have hired a new minister. Although she is sincere and hardworking, I feel I am not being fed by the new minister. What can I do to get my spiritual needs met? Several old-time members have moved to another church in the vicinity. I love this church and have many friends here. Shall I stay or find somewhere else to be fed spiritually?

— **J.S., via Internet**

Dear J.S.: Let me say this as kindly as possible. I understand the problem you are facing; you are not the first person to write about this. But I m afraid I have to disagree with your fundamental premise—the need "to be fed spiritually" by your minister. Adults feed themselves, my dear.

In the Unity way of thinking, as I understand it, you don't come to church to *get* a religious faith, you come to *create* one. Are you taking responsibility for your own spiritual growth by getting involved—working at prayer and meditation, reading the Bible and other inspirational books, taking classes, and volunteering to work in the church program?

Fact of life: Differences abound in all churches. You'll sit next to a person who prays and meditates two hours a day, and in the row behind you will be someone else who keeps no regular prayer schedule but is nevertheless "close" to God. Some people want very little Bible ("I left the XYZ church to get away from all that nonsense!"), while other people (like me) want most sermons to touch base with the Judeo-Christian Scripture in some way. Some people need lots of emotional connection with their minister ("God is love"); others need great ideas from the sermon (it's called New Thought, right?); and others just come because they love the music and frankly couldn't care less what the preacher has to say.

We say, "Oh, that's no problem! All people are works in progress. Who am I to judge? In Unity we accept people just the way they are."

Uh-huh ... does that include ministers, who are works in progress too? Doesn't it seem reasonable that ministers will differ as much as laypeople in their approach to life, love, God?

Here's the first lesson from *Dr. Tom's Unpublished Unity Basics 101*: "Keep Your Divine Appointments." God has brought you to this place and sent you this minister. Unless he/she is grossly incompetent, unethical or larcenous, may I suggest you tough it out a while and see what this very human person—who as you've said is "sincere and hard-working"—has to offer you? Perhaps she'll take you exciting places, to new spiritual lands where you'd never venture on your own. (Hooray! You think the Hebrews in Egypt really wanted that 40-year hike to the Promised Land?) Perhaps you'll offer her insights about how she can become a better clergyperson. (Sincere, secure people receive constructive suggestions as gifts from heaven.) And perhaps that could be precisely why God has sent her to you—and you to her.

> Dear Tom: I am interested in learning more about the study of metaphysics. Can you recommend a reading list for beginners?
> — **G.C., New Hartford, New York**

Dear G.C.: I like the "classics" on my shelf: Eric Butterworth's *Discover the Power Within You*, H. Emilie Cady's *Lessons in Truth*, and Charles Fillmore's *Christian Healing* are good places to start. Read anything you can get by Catherine Ponder and James Dillet Freeman. For a good introduction to modern Bible study, try a book by a friend of mine, Alden Studebaker's *Wisdom for a Lifetime: How to Get the Bible Off the Shelf and Into Your Hands*.

Avoid the temptation of "channeled" works, which you will find published by organizations other than Unity House. Stay with solid, Christ-centered metaphysical teachers like these, and you'll find the road ahead to be friendly and full of delightful surprises.

Don't forget the greatest metaphysical book of all, your Bible. If you read every biblical story as a metaphor of your spiritual growth, the mysteries unfold effortlessly. Never doubt one fact—God will be with you every step of the way!

> Dear Tom: For the past few years I have been searching for a metaphysical interpretation of the cleansing power of the blood of Jesus. What is

meant by the "washing away of sins with the blood
of Jesus"?
— **N.E., Memphis, Tennessee**

Dear N.E.: I would recommend studying the passage in
historical context to understand the significance of animal
sacrifice in the ancient world, which all this "blood of Jesus"
business capitalized upon when the early church was trying
to explain why its messiah got crucified. Not just Jewish
priests at the Jerusalem temple but priests and priestesses at
countless pagan temples offered animal sacrifice to right the
balance between heaven and earth. It was natural fit when
Paul and others decided that Jesus represented a "lamb of
God" whose death restored the balance of the whole world.

Metaphysically—which really means *symbolically*—blood
can signify *life force*. When people allow their indwelling
Christ to emerge, the rising tide of consciousness sweeps
before it all impure, lesser thoughts. Gone are fears and
doubts, anxieties and petty grievances. Sin is error belief, and
when the divine life force flows from within us, no error can
stand its mighty tide.

How's that for a metaphysical refurbishing of an otherwise
grisly text?

Dear Tom: I read a lot of the Unity publications,
from *Daily Word* to *Unity Magazine,* and I still have
a hard time trying to shift my mind to more positive thoughts. I battle between the New Thought

approach of happiness and abundance and the mainstream Protestant thought of having to deal with your struggles in life and that God is not a genie or Santa Claus. How do I deal with all the conflicting teachings out there to arrive to a better peace of mind?

— R.L.E., Wichita, Kansas

Dear R.L.E.: Christian metaphysics isn't magic, and God isn't Santa Claus. God is much, much better than St. Nick, who only gives good things one day a year. God is continually attempting to shower us with good things, which we in our ignorance are continually rejecting. Not only do we have a right to happiness and abundance, *it is our obligation*. As I have quoted earlier in this volume, Charles Fillmore said that it's a sin to be poor.

Hidden inside this seemingly outrageous statement is great, deep wisdom. We are not here to suffer. It is our moral responsibility to be happy and to enjoy the abundance God has in store for us. To accept less is to reject our birthright, which unfortunately too many people are inclined to do, often because of the extreme circumstances in their lives. But life will not get better for this suffering world unless we have a vision of prosperity and wholeness, which is possible for everyone. It is this poverty consciousness which drags humanity down, and that, my friend, is both a sin and a shame.

Now let me don my professor of theology hat. You have rightly identified the main difference between Unity's theology and some ideas found in what you called main-stream Protestant thought. More traditional Christians tend to see humanity as broken, unable to fix itself without divine intervention in the person of Jesus Christ. Some traditions call this original sin, but the moderate-to-liberal churches which constitute "mainstream" Protestantism tend to define the problem in terms of human tendencies to choose evil instead of good. This is probably another of my typical over-generalizations, but it's been my observation that conservative churches tend to speak of sin as individual choices to do individual acts: Sin for Christian conservatives is lying, cheating, committing adultery, killing, stealing—specific bad things which people do. However, moderate and progressive churches tend to see sin as institutional states: Sin for Christian liberalism is racism, sexism, homophobia, war, poverty self-centeredness, greed, cruelty to neighbor, despoiling the environment—negative conditions in social consciousness.

Transferring this debate to the realm of prosperity think-ing, conservative churches tend to see nothing particularly evil in having wealth and property as long as you don't use it for evil purposes, whereas progressives are somewhat suspi-cious of wealth precisely because their definition of evil is an institutional misuse of power. It is therefore not surprising when some liberals feel somewhat guilty about raising money, even for worthy causes, while some conservatives regularly post their offering-plate receipts, demand tithes from members, and feel great when their minister is success-ful enough to drive a Lincoln.

How to answer both extremes? Like some Unity thinkers, I would reply with denial and affirmation: *A second grader isn't a broken college student. People aren't broken or evil—they're incomplete, meaning they haven't realized or demonstrated their inner perfection yet. Life is a school, and lessons must be learned, but sooner or later we shall realize that we are One with all things in God, the One Presence/One Power.*

> Dear Tom: Can you tell me the metaphysical interpretation of Acts 17:27-28 RSV? It reads: "Yet he is not far from each one of us, for 'In him we live and move and have our being', as even some of your poets have said, 'For we are indeed his offspring.'" My references state that some scholars understand the first saying to be based on Epimenide of Knossos (sixth century B. C.) and that in the second one, Paul is quoting from Aratus of Soli, a third century B.C. poet from Cilicia.
> — **J.M., Utica, New York**

Dear J.M.: Actually, very little metaphysical "interpretation" is required, because the text is straightforward and metaphysical. In this well-known passage, Luke (the probable author of Acts) casts the apostle Paul in the role of preacher-teacher to deliver a message of universal salvation to the Greeks at Mars Hill. Paul begins by coyly remarking, amid all the statuary in that open-air temple of religious thought, that Athenians are highly religious people, because of their various shrines to the gods. He then mentions an altar erected "to an unknown god" and links this mysterious deity to the one true God, who sent Jesus Christ to bring the message of new life to the world. This has been the orthodox Christian interpretation, and it is correct.

However, the text also carries certain implications for human life that have not been popularly proclaimed by religious leaders. If we all "live and move and have our being" in the Divine, then God is the One Presence/One Power in control of the very foundations of reality itself. And if "we are indeed his offspring," we share a common bond with Jesus Christ and have the same capacity to express the divine within us. This deeper, metaphysical sense of these quotations has been more or less ignored through the centuries, because the implications of equality with Jesus have been too frightening for a lot of Christian thinkers to entertain.

Yet here we have a major biblical author (Luke) invoking the authority of another enormously important, first-generation biblical author and Christian missionary (Paul) to proclaim to the Greco-Roman world that we dwell within the Divine and the Divine dwells within us. Although time has proven that Luke's emphasis on the impending end and judgment of the world was a little hasty, the passing ages have seen a growing number of Christians returning to the mystical-metaphysical strains in Luke and Paul to discover themes like these, which have been ignored for too long.

Dear Tom: What is "ontology" and how does it pertain to today?
— **D.S.C., Roanoke, Virginia**

Dear D.S.C.: *Ontology* is the "study of being," which is also one of the definitions of metaphysics. The "M" word has fallen out of favor in philosophical and theological circles, although some of the categories of metaphysical thought survive in ontology. Arguably the greatest ontologist of the 20th century was Paul Tillich, who echoed New Thought metaphysics on several fundamental points. For example, Tillich said that God is not a being, God is Being Itself. If that sounds like a line from Charles Fillmore to you, you will begin to see the similarities.

Information on Tillich is easy to locate online. The best-known Tillich interpreter was John A. T. Robinson; try his classic book *Honest to God*. There's also a chapter devoted to Tillich in my book *Friends in High Places*. Both are available through online bookstores.

Dear Tom: I would like to know more about metaphysical Bible interpretation. I have read some books on metaphysical interpretation by Emmett Fox and liked them. I always wondered, though, how did the writers of the Bible have the consciousness metaphysically at that time? Also, what is your

personal opinion of how the Bible should be
interpreted?

— M.H., via Internet

Dear M.H.: You have raised an excellent and somewhat controversial question about *hermeneutics*, that is, the practices and principles of scriptural interpretation. Is "metaphysical interpretation" of the Bible—which is essentially trying to find allegories and symbolism in the text—a valid way of looking at sacred Scripture? Some people say that reading the Bible "metaphysically" is a way to unlock the true, hidden, secret meaning of the text. Others contend that reading the Bible allegorically merely superimposes whatever theology the reader brings to the passage, and that metaphysical interpretative principles require the readers to pretend that their 21st-century New Thought theologies are somehow hidden in the text of a 3,000-year-old document.

In biblical hermeneutics, the technical term for making the Bible say whatever you want is *eisogesis.* The word comes from a Greek expression which means "reading into" the text. Let's see if we can find a middle ground between the "hidden, secret key" party and the people who call metaphysical allegory nothing but biased eisogetical speculation.

Good metaphysical interpretation always begins with *exegesis,* another excellent Greek term, which means "reading out" of the text. Exegesis proceeds by looking at the *biblical theology* behind the text and asks, What was this author probably saying to the target audience? Biblical theology tries to arrive at the theology actually expressed in the Bible, taking each part as separate compositions by authors with widely divergent points of view. For example, Matthew's Jesus insists that his followers should keep all the Jewish law, but Luke's Jesus frequently reaches out to Romans and other non-Jews, and Paul tells his gentile converts they are not required to follow the Law of Moses. This is not really a contradiction because the Bible—which means "the books"—doesn't have a point of view any more than a library does. The Bible is an anthology of writings, not a single composition, and it logically follows that various contributors to an anthology will see things differently.

Now, about metaphysical interpretation ... As already mentioned, a "metaphysical" reading of the text is really a type of allegory. In allegorical interpretation, the reader attempts to discover deeper meanings in the symbolism of objects and events in the story. To use a modern analogy, Luke Skywalker's struggle against Darth Vader in the *Star Wars* movies can be seen as an allegory for the perennial battle over values and power between youth and parents.

Metaphysical interpretation of the Bible looks for even more personal meanings, because every person, place and thing in the text is seen to be a symbol of each person's spiritual growth. Some of the best metaphysical interpreters—like Eric Butterworth—deftly blend historical research, creative thinking and intuitive insight in their writings. The idea is to examine the names of persons, places and objects in a biblical passage, study their linguistic roots in Greek and Hebrew for alternative meanings, and come up with imaginative possibilities.

Are the conclusions you will reach the "hidden, secret" meaning of the ancient text? Probably not. At a public forum

in the early 1980s, I had the opportunity to ask the great biblical scholar Krister Stendahl if he thought allegorical interpretation was a valid way to read Scripture. I was merely an
Army chaplain, attending a conference of bona fide scholars,
and every head in the room turned as I asked. Because of its
speculative nature, allegory is seldom done in mainline
churches these days and has fallen into great disfavor among
scholars. Ironically, the religious traditions which practice
allegorical interpretation today tend to fall into two radically
disparate groups, 1) the *Second-Coming-Judgment-Day-Is-Near*
fundamentalists, and 2) New Thought-Metaphysical
Christian churches.

Anyway, Dr. Stendahl was a tall, thin Swedish scholar with
a kindly disposition. He smiled and said with his delightful
Scandinavian accent, "Yes, it is a wonderful way of playing in
God's garden."

I invite you to join the garden party. Grab a copy of Charles
Fillmore's *Metaphysical Bible Dictionary*, get a modern translation of the Scriptures—Unity Institute generally recommends
the New Revised Standard Version—and go for it. Or, for a
primer, read and study Mr. Fillmore's *Mysteries of John* or
Mysteries of Genesis, or Elizabeth Sand Turner's *Let There Be
Light*. Or just do your own interpretation. Any number can
play.

Dear Tom: I have benefited a great deal from using
this affirmation: *There is only one Presence and one
Power in my life and in the universe—God, the Good,
Omnipotent.* There is someone in my life right now

> who would benefit from using it but is unlikely to try, without knowing the biblical reference that authenticates it. Do you know if there is such a reference?
>
> **— D.M.C., Nashville, Tennessee**

Dear D.M.C.: Hmmmmm ... let's see ... The best I can think of is Luke's account of Paul's sermon at Mars Hill in Athens, reproduced at Acts 17:28. Actually, Paul is doing a kind of proof-texting of his own from Greek philosophy:

> For "In him we live and move and have our being"; as even some of your own poets have said, "For we too are his offspring."

I could name a few others, but this is the best. The earliest reference I can find for the statement in Unity literature comes in a letter written by Myrtle Fillmore. "There is but one Presence and one Power, God, the good."[4] Ironically, Myrtle Fillmore was doing what I'm doing here, answering a question from someone who wrote to her. So I suspect she did not invent the term but was using an idea already current in early 20th-century metaphysical Christianity as she sought, in that particular instance, to comfort a mother who had recently lost a child.

-21-

Nature, Ritual, Symbol

Dear Tom: I am concerned about the future of this planet. Do we have a right, by overpopulating, to destroy God's creation? I would be interested in knowing how the Unity philosophy fits into the mess we are making of this world.

— R.D., Pennsylvania (no city provided)

Dear R.D.: From its earliest days, the Unity movement has sought a balance between humanity and nature. Charles and Myrtle Fillmore founded Unity Village—today, the world headquarters of the movement—not only as a spiritual retreat, but, at the time, as a working farm. Even today there are hundreds of acres at Unity Village which are relatively wild country, with extensive forests and lakes. It is common to see deer and other animals strolling across the meadows. I have personally seen abundant creatures—wild turkeys, foxes, raccoons, possum, skunks (yuck!) and even a few coyotes. One spring evening I saw a speckled fawn curled up under a shrub not 20 feet from the edge of the golf course.

Unity publications overflow with nature, poetry and pictures of God's world. Our emphasis has been on humanity as part of the natural order because we know the nature of all reality is divine order. So to answer directly: "No. We don't have the right to spoil God's creation. We are its live-in custodians." Population control is only part of a wise stewardship of this planet. Responsible people find the balance in their lives and live in harmony with the world of nature and the realm of spirit, for they are one.

Dear Tom: I have always wondered about the contact between trees and Myrtle Fillmore. I read somewhere that she really understood the benefits of trees and wrote on this subject.
— E.B.D., Kansas City, Missouri

Dear E.B.D.: No direct connection to trees, according to the sources I checked, although she had a deep curiosity about the natural world. Mary Caroline Page, who would later take the name Myrtle and marry Charles Fillmore, was born in Pagetown, Ohio, in 1852. Her parents considered her frail and sickly, so she wasn't allowed to run outside and play. They made her sit quietly and conserve her strength. Of course, like any child, Myrtle hated it. She would take her brother's books and sit outside under the trees to read voraciously.

Today at Unity Village, there is a small grove of trees with a bench where people can sit and meditate, read or just enjoy the shade. It's called "Myrtle's Grove." Since you're in nearby Kansas City, why not drive out and sit there, communing inwardly with God and remembering the gentle spirit whom we revere as the Mother of Unity?

> Dear Tom: I appreciate very much that you see ani-
> mals as creatures with souls. I found a good medi-
> tation for our pets on the Silent Unity Web site. But
> what about all of those unnamed animals we
> "use"? We eat them; we use them for animal exper-
> iments. I feel sorry whenever I see a truck with live-
> stock. How can I fight those thoughts of sorrow and
> pray for those animals? What does the Bible say?
> — **C.R., Ravensburg, Germany**

Dear C.R.: I hope you still feel this way after reading my reply. Every once in a while someone asks a question which I know is going to get me in a lot of trouble—even with some of my friends—if I respond with integrity. But the feedback I have received suggests that people have become accustomed to this column's occasional plunge into their discomfort zones, and most readers seem to realize by now that all comments made herein are the views of one theologian, not the official position of the whole Unity movement. So here goes.

I share your concern for the animals, especially those exploited or mistreated by humans. Factory farms, brutality for the sake of increased yield, abandoned pets, dogs trained to fight—we have not done well by all creatures great and small entrusted to our care by Divine Mind. And—while it's a stretch for me to believe every beetle in the garden is Gandhi's equal—yes, I believe at least some animals have souls, and we should pray for all living things.

However, I also believe that neither the abusive misman-
agement of nature nor a romanticized New Age vision of

ecology as a peaceable kingdom should drive us to react in the extreme. So with great respect for animal rights advocates around the globe, I must conclude that, while cruelty to animals is unconscionable, eating them is not. I do believe animals have spirit-force and perhaps the higher species have souls. But I also believe nature answered your question a long, long time ago. Humans are omnivores. We have evolved to eat both plant and animal foods. We are neither cruel nor unspiritual when we do so in the right consciousness. A perfect example comes from the indigenous peoples of North America.

In an act of sacred celebration for the success of the hunt, Native Americans ate the raw, still-warm liver from freshly killed bison. It was a truly religious event, a holy communion on the mixed grasses of the plains, because the death of the bison signified the survival of the people for another winter. All that was missing were the Words of Institution: "Take and eat. This is my body which is given for thee ..." How could this kind of meat eating be anything but spiritual?

Life itself feeds on life to survive. Every hopping rabbit is a predator to the green plants in its grazing zone. And the owl eats the rabbit, and the mountain lion eats the owl. However, nature seems to favor balance, not overindulgence. Creatures who abuse their environment sooner or later pay a terrible price for killing off their food supplies and despoiling the niche in which they have survived. Human cruelty killed off the bison and destroyed the lifestyle of the Native American, and the human family has paid a terrible price for this error in consciousness by the loss of a deeply spiritual way of life which could have instructed us all.

I pray whenever I eat, partly to thank God, partly to thank all the hands which brought the meal to my table, and partly to celebrate the life force in the plants and animals which have given themselves for my nourishment. Every meal can be a communion with the Divine as it is expressed through the plants and animals which we reverently consume and transform into human flesh.

Yes, we should continue to pray for all God's creatures, especially the humans. We should pray that we can express more and more of the Christ within us and live compassionately in a world which we treat with reverence.

Dear Tom: Striving for oneness with our Creator is breathtaking, and I have no problem there. Desiring oneness with all humans is difficult at best. Truth for me is, I don't want to be a part of their lives, or them mine. In fact, I find that from time to time I go out of my way not to have to be in such company. I look for the Christ within, but I find myself struggling.
— L.P., via Internet

Dear L.P.: I think you may be confusing *spiritual awareness* with being an *extrovert*. Some people prefer quiet, private lives. There are even natural hermits among us. Cultural differences also make some of us less comfortable with overt signs of affection. I'm Pennsylvania Dutch, and we Germanic types are generally not your touchy-feely-type people. I confess, one of the situations which makes me extremely uncomfortable is when, during a worship service or spiritual retreat, the group leader has everyone look a complete stranger in the eye and sing or otherwise proclaim how much we love one another. I always feel trapped, embarrassed, inauthentic. I know this is very meaningful to some, but I wish there were more options provided for those of us who are no less spiritual, but more reserved.

Compassion does not require everybody to gather in a group hug. You can "love your neighbor" without spending your weekends at his barbecue. My suggestion is to be very kind—as you seem already to be—and follow your natural interests. Seek oneness with God, and let Divine Mind handle the guest list in eternity.

Dear Tom: What does the cross symbolize? My church doesn't display the cross, but others do.
— **K.U., Frankenmuth, Michigan**

Dear K.U.: According to the *Metaphysical Bible Dictionary* the vertical bar of the Cross represents "the inner current of divine life," while the horizontal bar means "the crosscurrent of human limitation."

I understand the cross to be a marvelous symbol of One Power/One Presence, God the good. The vertical stands for God's power, which the ancients thought of as flowing down to us from heaven above. The horizontal bar points to God's presence in the world—horizon to horizon. Furthermore, the symbol of the cross represents faith in God's Presence and

Power despite the most adverse circumstances life can throw at you. Regardless of appearances, God is good, all of the time.

So the cross—especially the Celtic cross with its circle of eternity—is a perfect symbol for metaphysical Christianity. I hope more churches use it.

Dear Tom: Does Unity use the cross as a religious symbol?
— J.P., Golden, Colorado

Dear J.P.: Some Unity churches display crosses, others—perhaps a majority—don't. Personally, as I've said before, I think the cross is an excellent metaphysical symbol, especially the Celtic cross, which has the advantage of antiquity and a mystical significance that transcends the Christian faith. In fact, Celtic crosses are reputed to predate Christianity, some examples going back thousands of years. The horizontal bar represents God's Omnipresence, the vertical His Omnipotence. The circle in the center of the cross represents the sun disk and signifies eternity; the knots often displayed on the arms and sun circle indicate the interconnectedness of heaven and earth, showing that God's goodness permeates all things.

Effectively speaking, the symbolism of the Celtic cross translates the well-known phrase "There is only One Presence/One Power in my life and in the universe, God the Good, Omnipotent." So I vote for the judicious display of Celtic crosses in Unity churches to enrich the symbolism of our worship experiences with the deep, visual mysticism of this pre-Christian artifact.

> Dear Tom: I have been wondering why there are no sacraments served and no baptisms at my church, as required by Jesus? Other churches have sacraments the first Sunday of each month, and the church I was raised in offered communion every Sunday. I miss that service because it meant to me that God forgave our past mistakes and that we could start over trying to do better.
> — **C.S., Reno, Nevada**

Dear C.S.: Your question about sacraments requires a series of lectures and a textbook to answer properly. Let me try summarizing. For a lot of complex historical reasons, Catholic and Eastern Orthodox churches observe seven sacraments: *baptism, confirmation, the Eucharist* (the Lord's Supper), *penance* (confession and forgiveness), *anointing of the sick* (previously called extreme unction), *ordination* and *matrimony*. Since the Reformation, Protestants have usually limited sacraments to practices inaugurated by Jesus and explicitly commanded by him. According to some Protestant theologians, Jesus did this only in regard to the Lord's Supper and baptism (1 Corinthians 11:23-25; Matthew 28:19).

Most metaphysical churches started as lay movements, so at first there were neither clergy nor sacraments. For example, when Unity founders Charles and Myrtle Fillmore began their healing, praying and teaching ministries, people attended other churches on Sunday and gathered in Unity study groups later in the day. When the first-generation founders finally decided to hold Sunday morning services, they wanted to keep the liturgy simple and uncluttered with ritual. Hence, no tradition of the Lord's Supper developed. However, these seven functions are apparently so central to a living, spiritual community that some form of each has re-emerged in present-day metaphysical Christianity.

Baptism was adopted as name-giving or "christening" in many of our churches. Some churches offered a spiritual communion service, which can be found in Unity hymnals. I've also heard of "flower communions," to which everyone brings a blossom to exchange at the service. Arguably, the popular "burning bowl" ritual has replaced the high church sacrament of penance. We still do weddings and ordinations, and healing prayer has assumed the role earlier played by the rite of extreme unction.

However, I must confess—and this is controversial in Unity—I agree with you. When I was minister of a Unity church, I offered the cup and bread on the first Sunday of each month. We had two cups, one with wine and the other with grape juice. People came forward, took a morsel of bread and dipped it into the cup of their choice, symbolically reuniting the "body and blood" (metaphysically, divine substance and life) of Jesus Christ. Ingesting the elements is a marvelous symbol of God's presence in the outer and the inner world.

I see no theological problem with proclaiming belief in the "real presence" of the Divine within the Lord's Supper elements. God is everywhere—therefore, God is truly present in the cup and bread, and if properly understood, the mystery of the Presence can convey Itself to us through the sacrament of Holy Communion.

We share a common heritage with the Christians who have gone before, and we affirm that common bond when we celebrate the Lord's Supper. The sacraments link us with a long line of believers in the Christ within. I hope, as we enter the new millennium, more ministers will offer Holy Communion in light of our belief in the omnipresent God and our heritage as followers of Jesus the Christ.

Dear Tom: Please, I would like to know if it is a sound doctrine to carry dead bodies to the church with the idea that we are going to pray for them before taking them to their graves? What are we praying for, especially in the church, which is the body of Christ, when we know very well that the souls of the bodies we are praying for are gone already?

— O.U.J., Cotonou, Republic of Benin, West Africa

Dear O.U.J.: You have asked several good questions over the years, my African friend, and this is another one. I know a lot of people who are uncomfortable with coffins in the church, especially an open casket. However, there is no official "doctrine" that I can cite on this subject. Certainly we believe the bodies of people who have made their transitions are empty of the souls those physical forms once housed. However, sensitivity is required here, because this is really a pastoral question rather than a theological one.

Although we pray for the deceased at a funeral service, a memorial observance really isn't for the dead but rather for the living. The community or friends and family gather to say good-bye for now—to celebrate a life, not a death. Some traditions and cultures do this without any physical remembrances of the departed loved one; others display pictures and memorabilia; still others honor their dead by bringing the physical remains of their beloved to a sacred spot—a church, funeral home or some other community-accessible location.

I do not know what your traditions are in Benin, but I have no doubt that dedicated clergy around the world know how to minister to those who are mourning the loss of loved ones in a culturally appropriate and pastorally centered way that meets the needs of the living while honoring the memory of the dead.

Good Questions

-22-

Many Gods, One Path

Dear Tom: I have been treading various paths searching out spiritual understanding for quite a while—paths such as fundamentalist Christian, Eastern philosophy, Baha'i, New Thought, Theosophy, Hermetic philosophy, just to name a few. I can't seem to land in one place for very long. Is it dangerous to wander through the woods alone?

— **J.B., via Internet**

Dear J.B.: I wouldn't call it *dangerous* so much as *lonely*. But it's your path, and no one can tell you how to walk it. Not everyone is a joiner. There are some lone wolves who must wander the forests and ridgelines, staying beyond the edge of community life, for whatever reason. If that is where your guidance takes you, then that is where you must go.

However, if you simply haven't found a spiritual home yet, I would urge you to take a good look at metaphysical Christianity, which is one of the most inclusive and empowering spiritual paths on the planet. Sample some Eric Butterworth, H. Emilie Cady or James Dillet Freeman. Attend some Unity churches. Breathe in some of the friendliness and deep spirituality you'll encounter.

If that doesn't work for you either, I bless you on your path. Please know two things:

Not everyone who wanders is lost.[1]

God is with you every step of the way.

Dear Tom: Why do some people get so upset when discussing religion? I can't have a conversation with my co-workers, because as soon as I tell them I'm a student of metaphysics, they immediately tell me I'm lost and going to hell. People can discuss politics, sports, child-raising theories or educational philosophies like sensible adults, but when they get on the subject of religion, they go medieval on you—torture chambers for all eternity and demons haunting the dark woods of their lives. It's totally bizarre. Why are so many otherwise normal people so nutty when it comes to religion?
— **C.S., Boston, Massachusetts**

Dear C.S.: Nothing else rattles the four corners of the cosmos like a disturbing idea in the religious realm. We live in a mental world of our own construction, and if there are enough shocks to the foundation, the whole universe could come crashing down. People will defend their worldviews with irrational passion because they don't want to go through the agony of rethinking the nature of Ultimate Reality. It's easier to believe the earth was created 7,000 years ago, in six days and by the hand of God, than to confront the modern cosmos with its vast, terrible sweep of billion-year increments.

Yet there are those of us who seem to know instinctively that God is greater than any of our systems of thought, greater than our fears, greater than our superstitions, and far greater than our theologies, however comprehensive and philosophically sophisticated. God is greater than all these things—God is the One Presence/One Power that causes the cosmos to be, and this Presence/Power is absolute good, absolute love. If we can wrap our minds around that First Principle, all else is commentary.

Dear Tom: I live in Sri Lanka, where there is no Unity church. My husband and I split six months ago but got back together again after resolving our problems. He says God answered his prayers, because he has started going to a Catholic charismatic church; he prays daily, tithes and goes to other church services. A friend took me twice for a prayer service, but I didn't find it inspiring because many were speaking in tongues and rebuking the devil in church members. Someone in the congregation caught me by the hand and said there was something evil in my house. Yesterday, she told me that God spoke to her and said if I don't humble myself more to Him, this time something would happen to one of my children. To her the devil is as powerful as God, and he is waiting to destroy us. This goes against all my Unity teachings. My husband thinks God is an old man in the sky, waiting to punish us if we deviate a little. What do I do surrounded by a group like this? I am being driven crazy. Please give me an answer because my friend's comments have upset me.

— J.D.S., Sri Lanka

Dear J.D.S.: I visited Sri Lanka in March 2009 and found the people of that island nation to be some of the kindest folks I have ever met.

Most of us have experienced the discomfort that follows when a friend or family member becomes a religious zealot, although yours is surely an extreme example. The Unity response in your situation comes straight from church history: to keep the faith despite persecution, overcome negative thoughts with thoughts of love. The members of that group are not reflective of the faith taught by Jesus Christ. I think my colleagues among the Roman Catholic priesthood would be appalled by what your friend told you. Can you imagine Mother Teresa threatening someone by saying God will hurt her children if she doesn't accept her theology? It's not only ludicrous, it's enough to make a Jesus-person ready to abandon Christianity.

If I were in your situation, isolated and far away from a church community that is congenial to practical Christianity, I think I'd find some friendly, English-speaking Buddhists and study with them. Also, keep in touch with Unity through sites on the Internet, like Rev. Wayne Manning's clearing-house for "Other Unity Sites" at *www.unityofauburn.com /usites.htm*, or visit *unity.org*, which is the official Web site of the Association of Unity Churches International and the Unity School of Christianity. Meanwhile, find time to pray, stay centered in the Truth, and know that you are never alone.

Dear Tom: I have been fascinated with the similari-ties between Unity and Eastern thought. Isn't Unity a Westernized version of Hindu and Buddhist beliefs?
— **J.C., Chicago, Illinois**

Dear J.C.: I get this question frequently. Hinduism, Buddhism and metaphysical Christianity share points in common, but Unity is an interpretation of life based on the teachings of another Eastern mystic, Jesus the Christ. Meditate on his words (for example, the Sermon on the Mount or his parables, which sometimes sound just like Zen stories) and you'll see how profoundly "Eastern" he is. Maybe that's because Truth is One?

Dear Tom: What aspects of the "New Thought Movement" does Unity embrace? Please clarify.
— J.P., British Columbia (no city provided)

Dear J.P.: Unity co-founder Charles Fillmore defined New Thought as "A mental system that holds man as being one with God (good) through the power of constructive thinking." While not currently a member organization of the International New Thought Alliance, Unity emerged from the same New Thought mix of liberal Christian theology— notably, Ralph Waldo Emerson (1803–1882)—and the science of spiritual healing pioneered by Phineas P. Quimby (1802–1866) and his successors.

Although it began as a self-consciously theological movement—i.e., grounded inside the Christian circle of faith— New Thought Christianity was deeply rooted in the philosophical tradition of absolute idealism, influenced by George Wiilhelm Frederich Hegel (1770–1831). We have much in common with New Thought folks. Most Unity bookstores offer works by outstanding New Thought authors like Emmet Fox (1886–1851), R. W. Trine (1866–1958), or Joel Goldsmith (1892–1964). When reading these and other fine New Thought writers, most of us say a hearty *"Amen!"*

However, New Thought's relationship to Unity is more like a first cousin than a twin sister. The main reason Unity does not claim to be 100 percent New Thought is found in this evaluation of that movement in John Macquarrie's book *Twentieth Century Religious Thought*:

For an illustration of the influence of absolute idealism on American religious thought, we propose to go outside of Christian theology to a representative of the heterodox movement known as "New Thought." This had many sources, and was not specifically Christian but sought to express the truth in all religions. It sometimes ran into extravagances, but deserves to be judged by its best representatives.[2]

Some contemporary groups that claim to be New Thought are, in John Macquarrie's words, "not specifically Christian," whereas Unity is very emphatically a Christian church. For all its positive values, New Thought moved away from the Christocentrism of its founders and remains ambiguous about its connection to Jesus Christ; Unity has not followed suit. Without a trace of intolerance, the Association of Unity Churches International and Unity School are unapologetically Christian. Certainly, we believe that divine Truth can be found in other religions, but it is through the window of Jesus Christ that we see the light of Truth. If we speak of the movement adjectivally, such as New Thought Christianity, then perhaps the term is an accurate description of Unity's heritage, if not our current status. For more background, check my book *Friends in High Places*, especially Chapters 8-10.

Dear Tom: I'm curious: How can you be an ordained minister of Unity and also an ordained minister of the Unitarian-Universalist Association?

I never thought the two were compatible. Do Unitarians believe in the divinity of Jesus? Do they believe in an afterlife?

— E.T., Knoxville, Tennessee

Dear E.T.: Since many of my readers have asked about Unitarian-Universalism, I guess we should unpack the confusion. My situation is probably unique. Like my predecessor in this column, Marcus Bach, I grew up in the German Reformed Church, which became part of the United Church of Christ (UCC). As a young man, I explored many religious ideas and was particularly impressed with Reformed Judaism. Eventually, I moved even further from Christianity and for about eight years became a follower of the Baha'i Faith, to which I still owe a great deal of gratitude and hold in highest regard. When I wanted to come back to American Protestantism, I needed a religious community that would not require any belief formula. I wanted to discover my own religion. That's when I encountered Unitarian-Universalism.

Although "Unity" and "Unitarian" sound alike to some ears, they are distinctly different churches today. As your questions suggest, most Unitarians affirm the complete humanity of Jesus—the word *Unitarian* was chosen in opposition to the *Trinitarian* view that God was wholly present in Jesus Christ in some unique way. Believe me, I could spend a long time on these issues, but nowadays only theologians like me are interested in the details of ancient controversies. Unitarian-Universalism in its present form allows its people to believe whatever works for them—to assemble their belief system from the raw material of religious freedom.

I served as a Unitarian-Universalist minister on active duty as a military chaplain, working among Protestants, Catholics, Jews, Muslims and people of no religious preference. While in Alaska, I became active in a local Congregationalist church and was ordained by the National Association of Congregationalist Christian Churches, a group which has indirect ties to my childhood church, the UCC.

About that same time, I discovered Unity. It was like coming home. Unity shares a historic, albeit informal, connection with the Unitarian-Universalist Association through Ralph Waldo Emerson, to whom both movements look to as a theological founding father. The Reverend Ralph Waldo Emerson was an ordained Unitarian minister and essayist who inspired Unity co-founder Charles Fillmore.

I guess the reason I've summarized my spiritual journey here is to encourage those who are seeking Truth to never give up. It took half a life to discover an expression of the Christian faith that works for me, the Unity way. God is patient, like an autopilot working quietly in the cockpit as we veer off course, gently correcting our wandering flight plan, until we find the best route home. Trust this program called life, and you will see its spiritual dimensions stretching above you like a clear, endless skyway. No matter what name you affix to the path—Unitarian, Unity, Congregationalism or whatever—if it's a true flight plan, you will home in on the knowledge that all Truth is One.

Dear Tom: I know you say you're a Christian, but I have heard it said, "There are many paths, but one God." Don't you agree?
— **W.R.L., Spokane, Washington**

Dear W.R.L.: Yes. In fact, you can turn that statement inside out, and it still works. *There are many gods, but one path.* Religionists around the world have created the best models they could to express the utterly inexpressible majesty of God. People have historically made gods in their cultural image, because that's all they had. The path to Oneness with this Divine mystery is really the same; it is achieved through love, prayer, meditation, wisdom, study and many other steps. Guides along the way might be Buddha, Jesus, Mohammed, Moses or other selections of human-made avatar images. The route is nonnegotiable; the destination sure. *The guides are not the path.* They are road signs, bench markers, pathfinders. So let's walk awhile with Jesus, or Buddha, or Krishna. And I'll see you at the top!

Dear Tom: I would like to attend a Unity church, but the closest in my area are an hour away. I did find a church that leans more towards New Thought and was wondering if you could provide a comparison between Unity beliefs and principles and those of other New Thought churches. Thanks.
— **J.G., Washington (no city provided)**

Dear J.G.: All New Thought churches are similar enough that you'll probably feel at home. The difference is one of emphasis, not fundamentals. New Thought churches believe God is One Presence, One Power, Absolute Good. We also agree on the indwelling divinity within each person and the importance of prayer, meditation and the practical application of spirituality in everyday life.

Having said that, I feel there are some differences of emphasis. I think it's fair to say Unity tends to be somewhat more Christ-centered than Religious Science, which leans toward a God-centered interfaith theology. Unity also makes more use of the Bible and uses more conventional language to describe its teachings. All these comments are subject to local conditions. Some Unity centers never mention Jesus; some Religious Science churches read from the Bible and speak freely of following Jesus the Christ. And sometimes I think the Universal Foundation for Better Living, founded by former Unity minister Johnnie Colemon, arguably does a better job teaching Charles Fillmore than we do. (And they published the first edition of my systematic theology, *Glimpses of Truth*.) If I were in your place, I'd go and try the New Thought church. You may find the minister is perfect for your needs. If not, there are plenty of Unity sites online. And don't forget your individual prayer and meditation work. God is always available for direct consultation.

Next time, try what the late Rev. Hypatia Hasbrouck recommended. "I like to write a letter to God and slip it into the Bible to 'send' it," she said.

I was a student in the class when she described her divine postal system. It was one of the greatest straight lines anybody had ever thrown my way, so I raised my hand and said, "Hypatia, if you get a reply—I want the stamps."

She laughed. And like many who went before, her light continues to shine, for now I've told the story to you ...

Dear Dr. Tom: I hear a lot of people these days who say they are "spiritual, not religious." What does that mean, and what's your take on it?
— **T.M., Chicago, Illinois**

Dear T.M.: You know, I have this discussion regularly among my colleagues, and the jury is still out on which interpretation will prevail. Here's my spin on the theological issues involved.

First, the expression you quoted is used quite differently in the wider culture from the way it is invoked in Unity and other New Thought churches. It seems to me that most Americans who say they are "spiritual, not religious" are really calling themselves *nonobservant*, meaning they have no pattern of regular church or synagogue attendance. A person is born into a Jewish family, even raised orthodox, but does not continue membership in a worshipping Jewish community as an adult. The same could be said of nonobservant Catholics, Mormons, Lutherans or Baptists. The "not religious" part means, basically, "I am not a participating member of any specific community of faith."

However, a popular idea floated around these days among New Thought circles is that we have a natural mission field among the many people who have distanced themselves from traditional churches and are seeking a faith that is spiritual, not religious. One of the problems I have with this notion is that it is an oxymoron. I might be making a huge generalization, but I believe it begins with the self-negating premise that there is something inherently evil in the organizations of humanity that are dedicated to the Divine.

Under this kind of thinking, "religious" ideas are suspect, because they represent traditions, old ways. "Spiritual" ideas, on the other hand, "slip the surly bonds of earth and touch the face of God." But it seems to me that, if subsequent generations of God-intoxicated souls come to a nontraditional church to find God like we did, they'll need to locate markers laid down by others who've already explored the territory; they'll need a trail of settlements along the path to support their journey. Call it *church* or *community* or *faith* or whatever, this support network/system is the very definition of religion. God provides people; people provide support.

A better description of *religion* might see it as "a recognizable group of people with shared beliefs and practices about God, the divine, and/or Ultimate Concerns." This description allows for "religious" humanists and members of nontheistic faiths (such as Buddhism), who profess no belief in God, to have "religious" ideas about Ultimate Concerns, such as compassion, justice and social equality.

In recent years, *religious* has taken on a negative connotation when paired with words like *ritual, institution* or *dogma* (doctrine). However, to dismiss the word as simply characteristic of old thinking is to misunderstand the social and theological depth of a religious community. From the tribesmen in remote villages who practice folk medicines and rituals handed down through the generations, to the Pentecostal Christian speaking in tongues in Alabama, to the Shinto priest invoking the ancestors of Japan, commonly held beliefs and practices bind people together in communities of faith. That is religion.

Spiritual refers to something more amorphous. It has many definitions, some of them rather contradictory. Although some philosophers (Hegel) and theologians (Tillich) hold that the power of existence itself comes from *spirit*, the New Testament word from which the term is translated is *pneuma*, which actually means "air" or "wind" and by extension "breath." In popular religious literature, from Billy Graham to Joel Osteen, the word spiritual is invoked haphazardly to mean "things of God" or anything which is sacred, holy or transcendent. New Thought writers sometimes use the word *metaphysical* almost interchangeably with spiritual.

The word *spiritual* may refer to mystical practices by which the believer comes in direct contact with the Divine, or it may be the experience of awe and wonder which people feel under a starry night sky, whether they believe in anything transcendent at all. It often has an emotional dimension to it, although "spiritual studies" are practiced in virtually every religious tradition as the elders pass on their truths to the next generation.

Certainly, the two words need not be mutually exclusive. In fact, one could argue that "spiritual, not religious" is not only incorrect by definition, but I consider it an uncomfortably arrogant viewpoint for an open-minded tradition like

Unity. We are a *spiritual religion*, a group of like-minded believers who seek deeper awareness of the Divine Presence and Power in our lives and in our world. That is why I have said for years that Unity is "culturally Christian, spiritually unlimited." For me, God is both within and without. God animates the cosmos with divine energy—which Charles Fillmore called *substance*—and yet speaks to me in the silence of my thoughts.

Every day, as I look out my window at the lovely Mediterranean-style buildings and talk with the extraordinary people who work here at Unity School of Christianity, I feel blessed to be a part of a religious heritage that puts Spirit first.

Good Questions

ENDNOTES

Preface

[1]James Dillet Freeman, *The Story of Unity*, (Unity Village, Missouri: Unity House, 1978), 170-171.

Introduction

[1]David B. Keller, sermon delivered at First Congregational Church (UCC), Concord, New Hampshire, available online at http://www.concordsfirstchurch.org/sermon102807.pdf (accessed April 28, 2009).

[2]Heidelberg Catechism, available online at http://www.ccel.org/creeds/heidelberg-cat-ext.txt (accessed April 28, 2009).

[3]Charles R. Fillmore, "The Adventure Called Unity." Charles R. Fillmore is President Emeritus of Unity School of Christianity. His grandparents were Unity founders Charles and Myrtle Fillmore. Mr. Fillmore is affectionately known around Unity Village simply as "Charles R." http://www.unitycr.org/aboutunity.html (accessed January 18, 2009).

[4]Myrtle Page Fillmore, to Charles Fillmore, dated September 1, 1878, transcript in the hand of Myrtle Page, Unity School of Christianity Archives, Unity Village, Missouri.

[5]An excellent primer on the Wesleyan Quadrilateral is *How to Think Theologically* by Howard W. Stone and James O. Duke, available at any online bookstore.

[6]Charles Fillmore, "About Unity's New Building," *Unity Magazine*, January 1906, 31. Brackets added.

Chapter 1: Letters From the Edge of Doubt

[1] Isaac Newton, quoted at Oklahoma State University Department of Mathematics Web site "Famous Mathematics Quotes" page, http://www.math.okstate.edu/~wli/teach/fmq.html (accessed March 21, 2009).

Chapter 2: Theodicy: The Primordial Question

[1] Harold Kushner, *Why Bad Things Happen to Good People* (New York: Anchor Books, 2004), 34.

[2] This letter was written years before the Wall Street investment debacle and the $50 billion Ponzi scheme by Bernard Madoff, arguably the biggest theft in recorded history.

[3] Marcus Aurelius, *Meditations*, Maxwell Staniforth, trans. (London: Penguin Books, 1964), 45.

Chapter 3: Wrestling With God

[1] Rudolf Bultmann, "The Mythological Element in the Message of the New Testament and the Problem of its Re-interpretation," available online at http://www.religion-online.org/showbook.asp?title=431 (accessed April 15, 2009).

Chapter 4: Prayer Problems and Possibilities

[1] H. Emilie Cady, *Lessons in Truth* (Kansas City, Missouri: Unity House, 1896), 12.

[2] James Dillet Freeman, "The Prayer for Protection," http://www.unity.org/prayer/prayers Affirmations/prayerForProtectionText.html (accessed March 27, 2009).

Endnotes

Chapter 5: Process Theology

[1] T.A. Kantonen, *The Christian Faith Today* (Lima, Ohio: C.S.S. Publishing Company, 1974), 98.

Chapter 6: The Soul

[1] Cady, 25.

Chapter 7: Evil Is a Four-Letter Word

[1] *New Advent Catholic Encyclopedia*, http://www.newadvent.org/cathen/02595a.htm (accessed April 3, 2009).

[2] Charles Fillmore, *The Revealing Word* (Unity Village, Missouri: Unity House, 1959), 25.

[3] Thomas W. Shepherd, "Does Religion Cause Violence?" *Contact*, Volume 42, Issue 6, December 2008-January 2009, 31.

[4] Fillmore, *Revealing Word*, 179.

[5] Cady, 44.

Chapter 8: "Hell, No ..."

[1] John Macquarrie, *Principles of Christian Theology* (London: SCM Press, 1977), 367.

Chapter 9: Holidays and Holy Days

[1] Howard Clark Kee, "The Gospel According to Matthew" in *The Interpreter's One-Volume Commentary on the Bible*, Charles M. Laymon, ed. (Nashville, Tennessee: Abingdon, 1971), 611.

Chapter 10: Imago Dei

[1] Others versions of the story are available online. One example is *The New Statesman* Web site:
http://www.newstatesman.com/200602130016 (accessed April 4, 2009).

[2] John 10:34-36, NRSV.

Chapter 11: The Bible for Postmodern Skeptics

[1] John 8:31-32, NRSV.

[2] Claude Holmes Thompson, "The Book of Jude," in *The Interpreter's One-Volume Commentary on the Bible*, Charles M. Laymon, ed. (Nashville: Abingdon Press, 1971), 943b.

[3] Alfred North Whitehead, *Dialogues of Alfred North Whitehead*, Lucien Price, ed. (Boston: Little, Brown and Company, 1954), 371.

Chapter 12: Lost Books, Lost Years—Found Now

[1] M.S. Enslin, "NT Apocrypha," in *The Interpreter's Dictionary of the Bible*, Volume I, George A. Buttrick, ed. (New York: Abingdon, 1961), 166.

[2] Gospel of Thomas, Saying 114, online source:
http://irupert.com/nagham/gospel.htm (accessed April 20, 2009).

Chapter 13: Parables and Assorted Goodies

[1] Howard Clark Kee, 634.

[2] Ibid.

[3] Didache 8:2, online at
http://www.spurgeon.org/~phil/didache.htm (accessed April 26,
2009).

[4] Emmett Fox, "The Lord's Prayer" online version,
http://www.aztlan.net/lordsprayer.htm (accessed April 20, 2009).

[5] Matthew 5:31-32, NRSV.

[6] Matt and Andrej Koymasky,
http://andrejkoymasky.com/liv/fam/biop1/paul01.html
(accessed April 26, 2009).

Chapter 14: God in the Hebrew Bible

[1] Exodus 7:16, NRSV.

[2] Exodus 21:22, NRSV.

Chapter 15: Reprogramming the Zeitgeist

[1] Charles Fillmore, *Dynamics for Living* (Unity Village, Missouri:
Unity House, 1967), 73.

[2] Charles Fillmore, *Atom-Smashing Power of Mind* (Unity Village,
Missouri: Unity House, 1949), 72.

[3] Luke 15:17-18, NRSV.

Chapter 16: Life, Death, Eternity

[1] Raymond A. Moody, Jr., *Life After Life* (New York: HarperOne,
2000), 11-12, 88.

[2] John 1:1-4, NRSV.

[3] Revelation 21:1-4, NRSV.

Chapter 18: Healing

[1] Hans Küng, in *Foundations of Theological Study: A Source Book,* Richard Viladesau and Mark Massa, S.J., ed. (Mahwa, New Jerysey: Paulist Press, 1991), 91.

Chapter 19: Prosperity

[1] Joel Osteen, *Your Best Life Now* (New York: Hatchette, 2004), 14.

Chapter 20: Odds and Ends

[1] Fillmore, *Revealing Word*, 200.

[2] Bhante Wimala is a magnificent person, a one-monk relief agency. Read more about him at http://www.bhantewimaLouisianacom/ (accessed April 25, 2009).

[3] I actually was a follower of the Bahá'í Faith for eight years, when I was a young man. You can read more about Bahá'ís at their Web site: http://www.bahai.org/ (accessed April 25, 2009).

[4] Matthew 13:57, NRSV.

[5] Myrtle Fillmore, *Myrtle Fillmore's Healing Letters* (Unity Village, Missouri: Unity House, 1954), 171.

Chapter 22: Many Gods, One Path

[1] Attributed to J.R.R. Tolkien, http://cs.nyu.edu/~dodis/quotes.html (accessed April 26, 2009).

[2] John Macquarrie, *Twentieth Century Religious Thought, New Edition.* (Harrisburg, Pennsylvania: Trinity Press International, 2001), 41.

Printed in the U.S.A.